THE MUSIC OF

FAMILY

AND ME

A MEMOIR

–

RICHARD VALANGA

BOOKS BY
RICHARDVALANGA

Complex Heaven
Complex Hell
Complex Shadows
Complex Reality (Trilogy)

Blind Vision
Day Of The Roman

The Wrong Reality
The Next Reality
Colosseum

The Sunderland Vampire
Bloodlust

The Last Angel
Blood Miracle

The Music of Roxy Music, Eno and Me
a memoir

The Last Butterfly (Children's eBook)

Front cover photograph, picture courtesy of Roger Chapman.
Inside pictures as indicated, courtesy of Roger Chapman.
Front cover photographic design by Richard Valanga.
Insert photographic details by Richard Valanga.
Apologies for the quality of my personal photographs, which were taken in the Non Digital Age of Photography.

This memoir is dedicated to 'good friends of mine'
Mick Averre and Steve Nanson

And my sons
Carl and James

Lay down easy, stars in my eyes...

Revisit, Review, Recall…

When I suddenly thought that I wanted to write about Family, I immediately decided that I would write it for my extremely talented bass playing multi-instrumentalist son James, explaining why Family's brilliant eclectic music is still so important to me. The answer is quite simple really, it is because of all the memories that the music evokes in me.

So the idea became a personal memoir but I knew that I would have to revisit not just every album but every song also, just to see what was ignited in those ol' memory cells of mine

It has been a great journey, well worth the ride back in time… and Family? Well they are still as brilliant as they ever were and that is no surprise to me as their music is timeless and years ahead of its time. Family produced music like no other; it is as simple as that.

Richard Valanga.

This album is dedicated
to all the people
who have pulled strokes
for or against us,
for they shall be called
fearless

Fearless
FAMILY

I am so proud to include this first response to my memoir

by Roger Chapman...

"I have to say I feel humbled in a big headed sort of way. Anyway, tell Richard it's great to read 50/100 pages of great reviews & I appreciate it very much. If he could send me some copies when published, I'll circulate to the people who I think & hopefully himself count. Again thanx very much, a real honour. Cheers Rog."

"Cheers & must say love the idea as it also brings me back long forgotten memories good & bad. - Rog."

Thanks Roger.

For
Roger Chapman
John Charlie Whitney
Poli Palmer
Rob Townsend
Ric Grech
Jim King
John Weider
John Wetton
Jim Cregan
Tony Ashton
and
anyone who worked with
Family

PRELUDE

There's a tall guy centre stage
Shoulder length hair and tattoos
Love hate scorpion
Smashing thrashing a tambourine to pieces
Against the mic stand
Lost in the music
In the moment
Arms suddenly pointing skyward
To another place another plane of existence
Head shaking wildly from side to side
A powerful creative psychedelic blues voice
That is full of soul and inner feeling
Completely unique and individual
It is a voice that can rock like no other
Yet can be so beautifully laid back
Cool and mellow when needed
A voice that really is an original work of art
And his presence and aura is amazing
Manic vicious and real
Not staged not acted
The mic stand is kicked aside
The tambourine broken and thrown
To the crowd who have joined with the singer
Dancing singing swaying
Violin saxophone good vibes wild vibes Polivibes
Dynamic unique original compelling
Guitar riff king and drum king
Strange band
Brilliant band
No other band like them
Never will be
Lay down easy
Stars in my eyes

1

The first rock record I ever owned was the Sgt. Peppers Lonely Hearts Club Band Long Player by The Beatles.

Christmas 1967 and a bleary eyed twelve year old wakes up early on Christmas morning, no birds are singing, no lights are on and the world is still and silent except for the dull snoring of sleeping parents. Do you remember those wonderful days, that feeling of excitement as you quietly crept down the stairs to see what was under the Christmas tree?

I have no recollection of any other Christmas presents that year, maybe there was a Johnny Seven gun, maybe a Man From U.N.C.L.E. suitcase, maybe I was now too old for such toys? But I still have a vivid memory of holding the Sgt. Peppers record in my hands.

The front room was eerily quiet, my eyes had not quite adjusted to the light and no fire had been lit yet, there was just me and my faithful dog Bengo and my very first vinyl LP record. It was a truly great feeling as I glared at the strange brightly coloured album cover, I had been a Beatles fan for some time and I also remember liking The Rolling Stones, The Who and The Monkees. I also remember having one of those Beatles plastic wigs, which thinking about it now; would come in quite handy for covering that small annoying bald patch on the back of my head.

That morning I probably did light the coal fire in the sitting room, it was something I liked to do; there was something about getting a roaring fire going, a sense of achievement, a feeling of pride even for a young lad. We lived on a working class housing estate called Pennywell, which was situated in Sunderland, newly built after World War Two to help accommodate the post war baby boom and I was one of those babies. I was even the 'baby' of the family as I had an older brother and sister. My brother John was a fan of the rock and rolling Cliff Richard I seem to remember and my sister Dot was a big fan of Elvis and my favourite rock band was the Beatles.

Me, me and my mother, me and Bengo, Bengo jumping over our garden wall.

The Sgt. Pepper album fascinated me then and still fascinates me today. The Beatles in multi-coloured military style outfits holding brass instruments, surrounded by an amazing array of movie stars, writers and sports stars; is there an artist among them? I do not know but this design was an early example of British 'Pop Art' by artist Peter Blake - colourful, bold, different and exciting... and mine. For me, Sgt. Peppers was where psychedelia exploded onto the scene. I loved the music and still do, my young taste in music had suddenly elevated to a creative new level then where the imagination of the mind held no boundaries.

First Family - Charlie Whitney, Harry Overnall, Ric Grech, Jim King and Roger Chapman. Picture courtesy of Roger Chapman.

And there were new British bands on the horizon that were waiting in the wings to challenge the popularity of The Beatles, bands such as The Rolling Stones and The Who, bands who had been heavily influenced by the American blues artists and these were Led Zeppelin, The Cream, Jethro Tull, Free, The Groundhogs etc., and of course Family, or The Family as they were known in the early days. Family were a Leicester band that had developed out of local bands like The Rockin' Rs (Roger Chapman's first band) The Strollers, The X-Citers, The Farinas and finally The Roaring Sixties and when they first arrived in London they had a gangster style image of 'mohair suits and new white spats' wide bold ties and Bogart hats. The American record producer Kim Fowley had commented that they looked like 'The Family' which was a reference to the image of the Mafia and the name somehow stuck. This image was to suddenly change though as the 'in crowd' became peace loving, spaced out hippies but Roger Chapman seemed to be at odds with this scene because of his short hair, his LOVE HATE tattoos on his fingers, his scorpion tattoo on his arm and his wild aggressive stage persona. Family had to move to London to further their careers and in the words of Roger Chapman; they were a band who just wanted to "turn the whole world on." Family immediately became one of the most popular live acts as this new style of 'underground' music began to really take off, Family were definitely one of the bands to watch out for.

I think that I must have been about thirteen years of age when I went into Sunderland city centre to buy my first Long Player vinyl record. At the time I did not know about Family, all I knew was that I wanted my own record bought with my own pocket money. I think it was the record shop known as Hot Rats or maybe the shop that would become Hot Rats where I made my purchase and the record I chose was bought purely because of the striking album cover art, a pinkish illustration of a large head with wide staring paranoid eyes, the mouth wide open as if it was saying to me, "Please buy me, please listen to me before it is too late!" The album of course was In The Court Of The Crimson King by King Crimson.

When I think now, I am surprised that I did not buy Electric Ladyland by Jimi Hendrix because at the top of my street, lived an older friend of mine called Ray Harrison and many a time I would pass his house on the way home from school and his bedroom window would be wide open with this Hendrix album blasting out at full volume, tracks like Voodoo Chile and All Along The Watchtower. I guess not many of the neighbours dared to complain about the loud sounds as Ray was the hardest lad on the estate and did have long hair, even the gang leaders of the local vicious skinheads were afraid of him. I did of course buy Electric Ladyland later and what an amazing album that is, Hendrix's best album for me.

When I arrived back home from the record shop that day, I distinctly remember my father laughing out loud when he saw the King Crimson album cover, I suppose the artwork was doing exactly what it wanted to do, it was getting a reaction. The music was definitely of it's time, magical, imaginative, and I remember it as almost a journey through a Tolkienesque landscape with a killer opening track, 21st Century Schizoid Man. It is definitely an album that I need to revisit at this moment of time and most surely I will have by the time you read this memoir of mine.

I think around about this time, I probably started buying the popular music press which probably meant a decline in my Marvel and DC comic collection – music papers like The Melody Maker, Sounds and The New Musical Express, all of which probably influenced my next vinyl purchase. I cannot remember exactly why I bought Led Zeppelin 2, rave reviews I guess but boy did that album hit a musical nerve within me. A great brown sepia print front cover of the band superimposed amongst what appears to be First World War pilots, a white cut out of the zeppelin crashing behind them. And the reddish logo type for Led Zeppelin was really captivating and I do have the hat and the t-shirt now as Zeppelin really were an amazing rock band that would easily withstand the test of time.

The album simply kicked-ass from start to finish, that blues element still there but now with a progressive hard hitting feel. There was also the hint of a gentle softer hippy style, a hint of things to come with What Is And What Should Never Be and the beautiful Thank You. This record and the start of the late sixties music scene definitely grabbed and shook me and wetted my appetite and my head thought *I want more...*

3

So my record collection now consisted of Sgt. Peppers, In The Court Of The Crimson King, Led Zeppelin 2 and the single Delta Lady by Joe Cocker if I remember rightly and I still have that single but what would be the next record that I would buy?

The importance of music to me and my friend's lives was now very obvious. We had started to grow our hair longer and by that I mean shoulder length, and I remember me and my school friend Ian 'Tiger' Caulder being told after one long summer school holiday that we would not be allowed to play for Sunderland Boys football team until we had our hair cut to that length. The main things that now dominated our teenage conversations as I recall; were football, music and girls of course. And one night, my good friend Mick Averre brought one of his older brother's albums around to my house, an album simply entitled Entertainment which was by Family. The majestic track The Weaver's Answer had not yet been released as a single and it was a track that would become a firm favourite with the Family fans and one that would reach a respectable Number 11 in the UK single charts

So Entertainment which was in fact the band's second album released February 1969 eventually reaching the heights of Number 6 in the album charts was the very first time I had ever heard Family. Mick told us that his brother Ken had seen The Family several times at The Bay Hotel on the Sunderland seafront. Mick said that Ken had told him that The Family had been unbelievably brilliant live and recalled the visual and vocal power of the lead singer Roger Chapman adding that Chapman was amazing to watch as he destroyed tambourines and mic stands as he freaked out to the music, he had even swung on Palm trees on the stage like some manic Tarzan of the Apes. *Palm trees in Sunderland?* I hear you ask, they must have been artificial surely?

Like Led Zeppelin 2, Entertainment blew us all away so to speak but there was something different about Family, it was not just guitars and drums, it was violin, saxophone, harmonica, piano and organ and of course the amazing vocals of Roger Chapman which were indeed an added instrument. This array of different instruments gave the band a unique and original creative diversity that continued throughout their recording career. Yes, I think 'unique' and 'original' are two words that describe the band best as noted by none other than the great John Lennon, but I will come to this later. After that night of Entertainment, I went straight out and bought the album and then I just had to buy Music In A Doll's House once I had enough pocket money saved up.

4

So what I would like to do now is drift back, to those lazy carefree days of my youth, to the spotty long-haired teenage days when the world was young and on the gleaming horizon everything was possible. My vehicle through those years is to be the music of Family, album by album, track by track and I hope that you will enjoy the journey too *as I re-enact the past,* as I try to describe each album and each song and what they meant to me. As I write this I am really looking forward to see what memories the music will no doubt unlock and I do think that I must apologise now to the relevant band personnel if I get the exact musical instrument wrong when reviewing the songs, the blend of music created by Family is so unique, sometimes it is hard for a non-musician like me to work out exactly what I am listening to.

MUSIC IN A DOLL'S HOUSE

July 1968

"They've got a fantastic blend in sound, the best I've heard for a long time." - John Lennon, the Music In A Doll's House launch party at Sybilla's in London 1968.

John Lennon and George Harrison at Sybillas. Picture courtesy of Roger Chapman.

I do remember being really excited as I put the Music In A Doll's House record onto the record player of the long radio cabinet at the back of the front room. This record player was behind my father's chair and his empty Vaux Double Maxim bottles and the Double Maxim bottle openers which were hung quite simply on a nail in the wall next to his chair for easy access. I still have one of those bottle openers on my key-ring now, so I suppose it has become a cherished family heirloom of mine and of course as the Scouts used to say, be prepared.

Looking at the cover of the album now, it gives me an instant nostalgic vibe. The front cover shows the inside of a doll's house and the various rooms within it from top to bottom, all lit up in yellow golden lighting. In those days apparently, a lot of the bands did all live together and Song For Lots and Coronation are Family songs inspired by this I think. I guess it was easier for the record company's to keep an eye on their potential stars this way, so maybe this design was in some way a nod to that.

Inside these rooms are the individual band members and initially it looks as if they have been superimposed into the doll's rooms but in fact I think it might be the other way round, the dolls have been placed inside real rooms or maybe it is a combination of both? Great graphic design that is an amalgamation of early Pop Art and pure fun by album designer Peter Duval. The front photography is by Julian Cottrell.

Top left of the doll's house we have lead guitarist John 'Charlie' Whitney, sitting on an ornate sofa in a bright red nightgown and sleeping hat, (and why am I suddenly thinking of The Marx Brothers?) Charlie is playing what looks like a silver banjo and sneaking a look at the door is a maid doll.

Next to this room we find bass player and violinist Ric Grech, sitting naked and cramped in a tiny wash tub, in front of a very finely dressed life size doll, who is obviously waiting for him to take her out somewhere.

Beneath these two top rooms, we have the middle floor of the doll's house, the stairway with marble busts and candle chandeliers and an adjoining room where we see the saxophone player Jim King, seated cross-legged on a large red cushion as if he is waiting for it to fly away with him like a magic carpet from the Arabian Nights. King is looking to an old vintage record player, maybe waiting for the sounds of Family to transport him to another realm. Another maid doll waits behind him.

Beneath Jim King's room, beside a wood burner, we find vocalist Roger Chapman, dressed in Davy Crockett buckskins, offering a cup of tea to a small weird looking doll, which I have to say that on closer inspection has the facial look of that horror movie doll called Chucky.

Finally, to the left of Chapman's room, we have drummer Rob 'Topper' Townsend, sitting comfortably in strange grey pyjamas and brown flat cap reading and enjoying the well chosen Topper comic.

So these were the first images of Family on their first Long Player and already I sensed that this was a band of musicians who did not take their own individual visual image too seriously, it was the music that mattered.

The back cover of the album compliments the doll theme perfectly; photography by Jac Remise and it does state that the album was published in THE GOLDEN AGE OF TOYS. On a lonely deserted farm road, sits a child size doll on an antique golden tricycle, the image reflected in the pool of rainwater beneath. I do find this a ghostly; gothic image which would have been even 'ghostlier' if this picture had been photographed at night. Actually, I do remember one reviewer (sorry, I cannot recall the writer's name or the article at the moment) commenting that there is a definite 'gothic' element to Music In A Doll's House and I have to say that I can relate to this. The reviewer did state that maybe Family were indeed the first Gothic rock band but I must stress here that I am not saying that Family were a 'Goth' band but I do think that there are definite 'gothic' elements to the music and lyrics of certain songs from the early albums which I will investigate as I go along.

Before Music In A Doll's House however, there was the single Scene Through The Eyes Of A Lens which was released in September 1967 and it does I think, feature original drummer Harry Overnall who was by all accounts, a brilliant musician, so Harry's departure from the band after this single is a bit of a mystery to me but I do have to say here that he was replaced by someone who was to become my favourite drummer, the equally brilliant Rob Townsend. I suppose at this point I should maybe reveal other drummers that I respect with the same level of admiration - Paul Thompson of Roxy Music and Lindisfarne, Simon Kirke of Free, John Bonham of Led Zeppelin, Henry Spinetti, John Lingwood, Patrick Carney of The Black Keys and the wonderful Mo Tucker of The Velvet Underground and so many more.

It would be years later when I would eventually hear Scene Through The Eyes Of A Lens though and it really intrigued me. Not to be included on Music In A Doll's House but it would have been perfectly at home there had it been included. The song starts slowly and quietly with Roger

Chapman immediately showing his descriptive genius, *Rainbows that sparkle like gems.* The song takes us on a trippy, shimmering descriptive ride then it explodes into a full on psychedelic beat with prevalent saxophones then just as suddenly it transforms into a 'James Bondish' adventure riff with a powerful beat. The B-side Gypsy woman is a more straight forward bluesy rock number that has a great sax break and this song shows us the strength and potential of Roger Chapman's vocals, a taste of things to come.

Early Family – Ric Grech, Jim King, Rob 'Topper' Townsend, Roger Chapman and Charlie Whitney. The only way is up. Picture courtesy of Roger Chapman.

For me, Music In A Doll's House is one of the greatest debut albums of all time, other great debut albums I have known are Roxy Music by Roxy

Music, The Velvet Underground and Nico, Led Zeppelin 1, Tons Of Sobs by Free, Naturally by J.J. Cale and once again I could add a lot more.

And like all great debut albums, Music In A Doll's House has a great opening track, as soon as the needle of the old gramophone player hit the groove, I knew that this was going to be another brilliant Family album.

2

Roger Chapman - Lead Vocals, Harmonica, Tenor Saxophone.
John Whitney - Lead Guitar, Steel Guitar.
Jim King - Tenor and Soprano Saxophone, Harmonica, Vocals.
Ric Grech - Bass Guitar, Violin, Cello, Vocals.
Rob Townsend - Drums, Percussion.

Produced by John Gilbert, David Mason and Jimmy Miller.
Engineers, Eddie Kramer and George Chkiantz.

The Chase
I probably did not quite 'get' The Chase at the time, a little too young and inexperienced in matters of the heart maybe. It is a song about a

woman who finally gets her man even though it was just for the thrill of it all, the excitement of the chase...

What is it now, there's something I see in your face
Feel like a fox, hounds close at heels at the chase

It has a terrific opening beat with a great typically understated Whitney guitar break followed by blaring saxophones and violin until the man is exhausted and has to give in to those fiendish womanly charms...

Hunted me out, sapped me of strength and of will

And the beat gets faster and ominous even, frantic as the shadowy horsemen get closer and closer...

Tally ho, tally ho!

A short opening song but a very important one, straight away the listener is bombarded by the strength and individuality of the unique Family sound, you know immediately that this is something different.

And the animal analogy within the lyrics is a theme that Roger would return to throughout his recording career.

Mellowing Grey

The second song on the album immediately displays a softer side to the band's music. The song floats majestically around the room as I listen to it now, immediately making me drift back in time to those laid back lazy days when romance seemed to be always on the horizon. The song has a dreamy hippy vibe, with hauntingly beautiful strings complimented perfectly by Whitney's gentle acoustic guitar.

Mellowing Grey is about an imagined love I think which Roger paints like an artist using the colours of his palette, *mellowing grey, Kingfisher blue, velvet shades, midnight blue and crimson charade.*

Another song that is lovingly compact...

All things within the world supreme
I compare with the love that is a dream

Two songs in and I am thinking, is this better than their Entertainment album? It certainly is a contender and it does sound different, maybe relates more to that Summer of Love, the 'Pepperesque' days... and that psychedelia was to increase with the third song on the album which took me back to the Saturday morning discos of my youth at the Sunderland Rink - Hello Goodbye by The Beatles, Pictures of Matchstickmen by Status Quo and Everlasting Love by Love Affair to name just a few. And me in my groovy brightly coloured Paisley patterned shirts, much too shy to ever get on the dance floor but I did get a girlfriend from the leafy faraway lands of Chester-Le-Street which was pretty cool for a young towny boy from the rough Pennywell suburbs, and I did get letters from her which I think I may still have somewhere. I remember her as a very pretty blonde-haired girl with great cool fashionable dresses; wonder if she ever got married?

Never Like This

Lyrically, Never Like This could be an accompaniment, maybe even a progression to The Chase and Mellowing Grey. The woman takes her man back home for tea to meet her parents, has she finally caught her man, maybe is she pregnant?

Been through this before but never like this the chorus sings.

A wailing echoing harmonica opens the track then suddenly jumps into a stomping steady beat with Rob Townsend drums prominent in the background accompanied by choral vocals and a ghostly piano...

And the girl with the faraway look in her eyes has suddenly become very important in life. How many times has that happened to us all?

Me My Friend

This track was Family's second single with the B-side being Hey, Mr. Policeman. I have seen a sleeve jacket for this single which has a very decorative design, orange background with a large FAMILY across it with black images of band faces beneath it. This is the first time that the famous FAMILY logo typeface was used and the typeface is P22 Kilkenny Pro and many thanks to Del Gentleman at Mojo Magazine for this information, I have been wondering what it was for years, I guess I always thought that it was a specially designed logo. The FAMILY logo was used on the brilliant 1969 single No Mules Fool which has the excellent A Good Friend Of Mine as the B-side. The FAMILY logo was to make its album debut with their third album A Song For Me.

Musically and lyrically, this is an unusual song and quite hard to categorise, maybe an unusual esoteric choice for a single but brilliant all the same.

Does it feature the same man and has he moved on with his life, has he left the girl with the faraway look in her eyes but is still looking for love? Is it some sort of confession about still wanting to discover new things, to be not tied down, to go on a voyage of discovery, even to the stars.

There is a great opening to this song with what sounds like a fanfare of trumpets and saxophones, accompanied by a dipping echo drum that is reminiscent of an Indian beat. Jim King opens the singing which becomes a duet with Roger Chapman.

The man is now reflecting...

I have seen many lands
I have been far and wide
I have sailed many a tide

And Chapman bursts in with ferocious, rasping vocals that crash through your mind, answering his own thoughts...

But I wish, me my friend, I could sail to the stars
Have the gift to transport
My whole being, my whole thought
To a world of dreams, my friend

This track really highlights the power of Family and the power of Chapman's voice. And once again the man is searching for true love before it is too late, a love that can only be found out there amongst the stars maybe?

The song fades into one of the three short musical interludes on the album...

Variation On A Theme Of Hey, Mr. Policeman

The band blowing, guitars riffing, harmonica wailing into...

Winter

A crashing piano echo starts this song with a guitar riff that is vaguely eastern again. Then Roger Chapman's powerful vocals tell the story again. The man is now in winter and he does not like it...

Wish that I could hibernate
Go to sleep and never wake

Strange wailing riffs prevail here with low saxophone, the instruments melting, blending then merging together until they are almost indistinguishable - violin, vibes, a ghostly background chorus then a violin solo that fades into the lonely harsh sound of just a cold wind blowing. I can feel this cold; hear that desolate wind whip across the moors, *Heathcliff, Heathcliff*... sorry, got a bit carried away there. See, that is what I mean by that gothic vibe. And an icy feeling of dread does surge through your body.

But only for a moment...

Old Songs New Songs

That journey through the winter wastelands of your mind is suddenly broken by slow moaning strings then a pulsating upbeat bass and loud wah wah harmonica crash in, that man is up to his old tricks again...

My girl there, she lies sleeping
The other door slips ajar and it's my wife
She's been peeping while I've been leaping

And the tempo picks up with haunting high pitched background vocals...

Old songs, new songs
Keep on singing

Chapman belting it out and the stereo sounds cross over in your ears as Whitney with his double neck guitar switches riffs, switches sounds, the band really blowing now. A saxophone blasts in the background then goes solo as the frantic dance-pace picks up with the sound of horns and saxophone and the vocal rolling guitar fights in your ears... nobody does stereo like Family did.

Old Songs New Songs was a single which was released in July 1968, the B-side was Hey, Mr. Policeman and there is a Youtube clip of the song from December 1968 from a French tv show where the band is joined on stage by some dancing chicks in checkered mini-skirts and leather boots grooving along to the Family beat.

While back on the album, as if to give you a breather from Side A...

Variations On A Theme Of The Breeze comes to your rescue... a distant sound getting closer, joins together with wonderful melodic background guitar and a tinkling piano and then sudden crashing organ, music to take you to those stars... and you want the Variation to be longer but you know the length of the vinyl is too restrictive.

Hey, Mr. Policeman

A slow bluesy beat starts this track with another wailing harmonica and clear crisp drumming. Once again there are haunting tenor and soprano saxophones as the laid back understated vocals bring you up to date with the man who now seems to be paying for his wayward lifestyle but he still wants to see that woman one last time but does she care for him?

Can I see her one time, before I make jail
I cared for that woman...
I cared for you woman
You call it a crime...

The saxophones follow and echo Chapman's lead then a clanging instrumental break, all the instruments merging until the lonely saxophone outro fades into…

See Through Windows

Suddenly the sound of a distant motorbike or maybe an aeroplane even taking off hits you, the music swirling around your head until a jumping rock beat breaks in, clear cut harmonica stuttering in time with the guitars.

Is the man in jail now?

See through windows, look at things
Eye's see life's meaning

And that harmonic in the background is wailing to that unique Family beat that has a vague eastern feel to it. Then a great spontaneous guitar break that sounds like the strings are going to burst at any time. And that haunting harmonica or is it saxophone? again that is now solo, going from ear to ear, stereophonic, until a stronger guitar picks up the pace, wailing, screeching into the start of…

Variations On The Theme Of Me My friend

And that now familiar eastern vibe floats through your mind making you drift away to new imagined places that you have never been to before…

Peace Of Mind

And the beat continues; the power increases. Does the man have peace of mind now or are things about to darken around him?

Take your time ease my mind
Wait until my thoughts are blind

I understand that Family used to finish their live set with this song and it is easy to understand why. Another stomping, haunting opening with great strong violin and strong Chapman vocals, *peace of mind* being echoed as Chapman sings it, the voice stereophonic… then a clear, acoustic guitar, the vocal harmonies becoming ominous, scary even, screaming, drum fever pitch…

Until
Stop
Then…

Voyage

That 'Family beat' continues; the Family power increases. The man's peace of mind no longer exists.

The lights in the Doll's House are flickering and darkening, is this the start of that gothic winter I mentioned earlier...

Is death approaching?

Haunting ghostly strings echo, and that spiralling sound, taking off in the background until the drums come crashing, rolling in...

Where do I look for proof?

Chapman spits out...

Horror, screeching, what is approaching?

As the music breaks into thundering drums, manic violin; the sound of paranoia... stop...

What is time within my mind

Is a red rose red to a man who is blind?

Crashing drums again.

Is the man dying, is death finally here?

Where do I look for proof?

Who do I ask and what do I say

As I sail on my voyage of truth...

The sound of death, screaming, tearing, haunting, cutting deep into your soul...

Until

A ticking, clicking... guitar being picked...

The Breeze

Who is the breeze, is it the ghost of the man himself or is it the spectre of death still lingering?

Nobody knows, nobody sees, I am the breeze...

Guitar plucking in the background as the sound of a clock ticks ominously.

The vocals floating, the guitar talking and still that tick tock beat while the violin floats behind it...

3 x Time

Lively saxophone opening...

There have been many blue yesterdays, pass me by

And as I sit here, my time goes fast

As I re-enact the past

Is the ghost reminiscing?

And the tempo picks up slowly, gliding through your mind...

Until you reach the final statement from the man...
The things I've done and all the friends I've met
Now looking back there's nothing I regret
That breaks into a wild celebration of all the instruments, party time, let's dance, almost music to take your clothes off to, if you get my meaning... bring on the dancing girls, swirl those sashes, and the music swirls suddenly, almost erotic, humming, building, those angelic vocals rising until...
A brass band crashes the party...
God Save the Queen
Fade...

Review

Music In A Doll's House reached 35 in the UK charts, not bad I suppose for a debut album and fifty three years later, the music still sounds as unique and original as it did then. The album is a powerful shining masterpiece, with music from another dimension, another plane of existence. Taking us to the stars on a voyage of discovery like no other. Underground rock, psychedelic rock, spaced out, freak out, stop start rhythms, incredible dynamics, voices and harmonies at times haunting, at times angelic, at times demonic. Saxophone, harmonica, violin, drums, guitar melding and merging together like a living thing, music with a life of its own. Eastern echoes at times, hippy, trippy, colours, *crimson charade* to *Kingfisher blue*, it's Van Gogh, it's Pollack, Pop Art, gothic, it's a journey through your mind, ear to ear, stereophonic, lost love, past love, future love, a doll's house reveals it's stories, it's secrets, *see through windows, look at things.*

And maybe I think now suddenly, that Music In A Doll's House was in some ways dare I say, a sort of concept album, the story of a man, his life, his loves, his journey, his death maybe? I guess only Roger will truly know the answer to this.

Paul Thompson of Roxy Music listens to it again, "I must say that I have really enjoyed listening to this album again! Fantastic songs, fantastic musicianship and to boot I'd say how amazed I was at myself remembering nearly all of the words! Mind you, I must have played it a few thousand times back in the day! Great album, great band and a massive influence on me. Love it, Love it, Love it!"

Phew; what a musical journey; what a debut album; confirming from the start, what a totally unique band Family were. They certainly don't make them like that any more and never will probably.

What other great debut albums have I enjoyed, what can I compare in terms of creativity and a unique new sound? I have previously mentioned Roxy Music's debut album which I actually bought purely because of the advertisement in the music press, I had never heard their music. Because of Family I was now looking for equally creative bands but I probably did not even realise this at the time. And like Family, Roxy Music were original, maybe more fashion conscious than Family because of it's art school members but straight away I knew that they were creating a new sound, an experimental sound inspired by it's ex-art students, Bryan Ferry, Brian Eno, Andy Mackay, Phil Manzanera and of course the creative heartbeat of Paul Thompson..

Like Roger Chapman, Bryan Ferry has a very distinctive voice and the songs are futuristic and nostalgic at the same time with similar ingredients to Family, saxophone, synthesiser, creative guitar and the incredible drum skills of brilliant drummer Paul Thompson who like Rob Townsend had a great sound to his kit and he had to deal with the difficult Ferryrhythms like Townsend had to deal with the unusual time signatures of the Chapman/Whitney songs. The only thing missing in comparison to Family was the violin but that would be added to Roxy Music later after the departure of Brian Eno, who was to go on and produce his own great unique debut album.

I remember that my friends at the time did not get into Roxy Music at first; it was with their next album For Your Pleasure and the hit single Virginia Plain where they came on board.

The reason why I am discussing Roxy Music here is because more so than any other band, I see comparisons between Family and Roxy Music and that is why I am mentioning them here at length. The song structures and dynamics on Family's Bandstand and Fearless are very similar for me to those on Roxy Music's early albums especially For Your Pleasure. And I do know that Roxy Music's members would have been aware of Family's music, especially Paul Thompson and Phil Manzanera, who have both stated that they were fans of Family. I wonder if Bryan Ferry was? It would be interesting to know also, if Brian Eno was aware of the pioneering electronic keyboard work of Poli Palmer on the Bandstand and Fearless albums which I find very 'Roxyesque' or maybe it is the other way round and Eno's Roxy work is at times very 'Poliesque?'

Two great bands then, two great debut albums and two great catalogues of music.

Family, Hyde Park 1969; supporting The Rolling Stones.
Picture courtesy of Roger Chapman.

Family, Hyde Park 1969; supporting The Rolling Stones.
Picture courtesy of Roger Chapman.

Family, Hyde Park 1969; supporting The Rolling Stones.
Picture courtesy of Roger Chapman.

March 1969

"Some argue that this record is the birthplace of progressive rock such is the invention and vision on show." - Jim Irvin, Mojo Magazine, August 2021.

1

So back to my council house in Sunderland and Family's second album, Entertainment and a slight switch in style and feel maybe compared to Music In A Doll's House or maybe it is the start of a natural evolution in musical creativity.

And what did I think of the album cover back in those days? Compared with the bright illuminating image of Music In A Doll's House, we have a starker black and white cover but there is still that feeling of fun never the less. FAMILY ENTERTAINMENT in bold white capital lettering at the top under which is a strange gathering of what at first appears to be circus personnel - a naked lady in a large open ended drum, who is about to be hit on her bare bottom with a drum stick by a tall long-haired lady in vintage aviator glasses, a small man beneath her is looking up to her while holding a small doll which could be a slight reference to Music In A Doll's House.

Lying on the floor with his legs half bent up in the air is a circus strongman, complete with an outrageous long curled moustache, fist clenched, his face smiling as he holds the strange trio above him. This is family entertainment but not as we know it. The curious album design was by Alan Aldridge and the photographs for the front and back by Rodger Phillips.

On the back cover, we find stark half portrait profile portraits of the band, looking reflective and a little intense as their faces fade ominously into the black background, creating an almost ghostly image of the band that once again suggests a vague gothic vibe to me. Is the mood of this album going to be dark or foreboding or will there be a light reprieve as the front cover suggests; maybe a strange night of entertainment is in store for the listener.

I am now thinking back again, trying to remember what it was like when the record player clicked into action and the opening track started. This is me hearing Family for the first time all those many years ago.

2

Roger Chapman - Vocals, Percussion.
John Whitney - Guitar, Piano, Organ.
Jim King - Tenor and Soprano Saxophone, Harmonica, Piano.
Ric Grech - Bass Guitar, Violin, Vocals.
Rob Townsend - Drums and Percussion.

The Heavenly Strings arranged by Tony Cox.

Produced by John Gilbert and Glyn Johns.
Engineer, Glyn Johns.

The Weaver's Answer

Weaver of life; let me look and see.

A lonely violin starts and a reflective passive voice asking the Weaver of Life to show the images and patterns of his life on some mystical tapestry (is it that man from Doll's House again?) Then thumping drums in the distance getting closer, a single lonely flute with clicking castanets.

And the music gets clearer, louder as the beat gets into a groovy rock beat, bass singing, manic flute in the background and Chapman, bold then gentle then growling in intensity into a bold saxophone break, bass rocking along showing the skill of Grech, King's saxophone singing now as the music builds behind until Whitney's wailful guitar break which is perfect for the song, Townsend's drums crashing all around.

The man is now looking at the tapestry, angry as he realises that death is approaching...

After days of wondering I see the reason why
You've kept to this minute for I'm about to die

And the end is gentle as the flute and violin and plucking guitar fade out...

A gothic story that Edgar Allan Poe would have been proud to pen and listening again, it easy to see how this became Family's anthem. Is there a better opening track? It is one of those songs that you never ever tire of, in fact I never tire of any of Family's songs and I have gone on record in the Family With Roger Chapman Appreciation Society Facebook page that there is not one single Family song that I do not like.

If you were to ask the Family fans what their favourite song is, then I am pretty sure that the majority would say The Weaver's Answer. However, I have to confess though that it is not mine, I think it suffers from what I call the 'single syndrome,' meaning the overplayed single, the overplayed song, a bit like why I like Free's 'Alright Now' much more on Free Live than the studio version. The Weaver's Answer is obviously right up there for me and is one of the greatest rock songs I have ever heard but my favourite song is on an album that we will come to later and that shows to me how Family continued to consistently create and evolve from album to album, sometimes under adversity due to line-up changes which obviously affected the band's sound. In terms of band members, I see the albums of Family in sets of two with different personnel...

Music In A Doll's House / Entertainment - Grech / King.

A Song For Me / Anyway - Weider / Palmer.

Fearless / Bandstand - Wetton / Palmer.

It's Only A Movie - Ashton / Cregan.

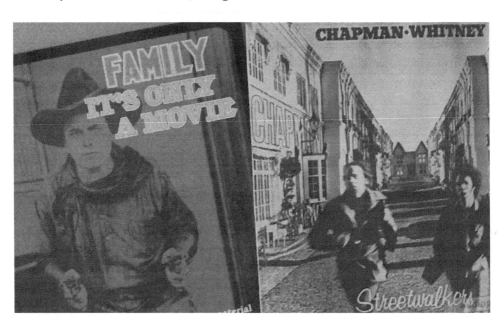

And finally of course, Streetwalkers - Chapman / Whitney.
   And I have always thought that basically the Chapman/Whitney Streetwalkers album would have probably have been the next Family album and what a fantastic album it is too and I will discuss the album and the memories surrounding it later.

So for me, you are not going to get a better opening track than The Weaver's Answer. All the elements that make up Family are there, the strength of Roger Chapman's vocal range, intense violin and strings, bold clear saxophone, beautifully creative guitar and bass, all held together with the superb precision drumbeat of 'Topper' Townsend. After this track, I knew that Family were now undoubtedly my favourite band and I still had the rest of the album to look forward to.

In 1970, The Weaver's Answer was released as a single with the B-side being Hung Up Down, both were remixes of the Entertainment songs, mainly because the band were never happy with the production mix of Entertainment which was produced without them knowing while they were out on the road. This would lead to the compilation album Old Songs New Songs further down the line, an album which would include new versions of some of the Entertainment songs, remixed by the band. Also on the B-side was a new song called Strange Band which would find itself on the live side of the album Anyway.

Strangely enough, the jacket cover for The Weaver's Answer single release would be called **strange band**, bold white type out of a red background and underneath the FAMILY logo. At the bottom of the cover are the band; Roger Chapman smoking, Charlie Whitney smiling and in between them is new member John Weider with an outrageous green face looking like The Incredible Hulk with long hair, a thought bubble coming from him with the single word ANYWAY. The back cover shows Family's three albums to date next to a great iconic white image of Chapman singing into the mic.

The single reached number 11 in the UK charts and looking at my single now, it seems to be a misprint, as both sides indicate the B-side details, maybe it could be worth something now to a serious collector as an oddity but I would never part with it.

Observations From A Hill

I did read somewhere that it is Jim King on lead vocals on this track but King is not credited with vocals on this album so I assumed that it was Ric Grech singing who is credited but thanks to the feedback from Roger Chapman and Simon Boxall, I now know that it is Jim King. Roger Chapman would sing the lead vocals on the Old Songs New Songs remix and here we find Roger standing on a hill observing the myriad of daily life below...

People are strolling, cars only rolling
Down man made paths of grey stone

Maybe a Sunday stroll out in the countryside inspired this song...
Church organ, choir sing hymn life
Sunday eve quarter past five
And then he sees someone below he knows, a woman beckoning him to follow her but does he?
Maybe I'll come down tomorrow
Acoustic guitars open the song with a country-style "Yahoo!" then violins and Grech sings quite deadpan above a jaunty, up tempo beat. Chapman bursts in on the chorus adding immediate power to the song...
These are observations from a hill
Then a violin, staccato and flowing and Whitney's echoey guitar. The swaying violin leads the song out with that now familiar Family style ending that beckons you to want more.

I am pretty sure that it was The Weaver's Answer that inspired me to take up violin lessons at school, man I was so crap at that instrument, they put me in the third violins section of the school orchestra and I remember that all I used to do was look at which way the other violin bows were moving, up or down, when we had to play in school assemblies, (Laughing Emoji) Eventually they gave me the boot and boy was I relieved but it still did not stop me loving the instrument and the way Grech and Weider played it. Later on I was to appreciate the avant-garde sound of John Cale's Velvet Underground viola and then the magnificent strings on his brilliant Paris 1919 solo album.

Hung Up Down

And the beat gets heavier.

I saw Roger Chapman live in Newcastle in 2018 and I must confess that I was a little bit worried about the possibility that the voice of a then 76 year old could be finally beginning to fade somewhat (and I do remember reading that at some point Roger did have a career threatening throat condition) but I have to say here that I was most pleasantly surprised, 'The Voice' was still strong, still compelling, still brilliant and vibrant. Chapman did refer to the power of his voice in the August 2021 edition of the Mojo magazine saying that "When I was young, I had 300%, now it's down to about 90%" and that ain't bad for a 79 year old as his latest excellent album Life In The Pond testifies to. The album is currently getting rave reviews as I write this and generating widespread interest as Chappo re-emerges in the music press and on the radio again.

And talking about power, I really have to mention here that the start of Hung Up Down really blew me away in Newcastle. I was standing at the side bar to the left, looking towards the stage and the power and force of the opening to the song was unbelievable so credit to those amazing musicians backing Chappo that night. I have seen many live bands over the years in various locations, inside and out but I cannot remember feeling such immense visceral power, I felt it surge through my body like a massive invisible wave as it shook the very foundations of the hall.

There is a slight acoustic intro then a deep plucking bass backed by a swirling violin...

What the hell...

Chapman's vicious ferocious vocals; and he is angry about those lying politicians...

So who's to cry, politician's lie
When you know damn well they do

Choppy guitar behind Chapman's vocals.

And he's still angry...

While men who count large bank accounts,
make wars for their own ends

Chapman screaming, wailing at the end as the song fades. Hung Up Down is one of the great rock songs and it was a real privilege for me to see and hear it in 2018 after all these years of listening to it, to really hear the power of the song live.

Summer '67

On just about every Family album, there is an instrumental, a chance for band members to display their versatility, musicianship and skill. On Music In A Doll's House it is the Variation interludes, on A Song For Me it is 93's ok J, on Anyway it is Normans, on Fearless it is Crinkly Grin, on It's Only A Movie it is Banger and on Entertainment it is this song, the odd man out being Bandstand.

Summer '67 is a John Whitney composition which opens with a jangling guitar fading in then you hear strings, a very orchestral sound. You could be on that magic carpet, back to that Summer of Love, off over those Arabian or Indian landscapes. I can even imagine those masked belly dancing girls in those hot tents, actually there is a Youtube video of women actually belly dancing to Burlesque, weird.

Then we hear a pizzicato style violin, high saxophone, a dreamy rhythm with an intriguing drumbeat as we go back to the main eastern theme with everything fighting for attention in the background. It is music that does transport you to another place, somewhere exotic, almost erotic in the way that it hypnotizes you and you wonder what other musical delights await you next on this amazing album.

How-Hi-The-Li

How-Hi-The-Li is the first of three Ric Grech songs on the album and I believe he is also co-credited with Chapman and Whitney on the last track Emotions. I have spotted a misprint on the cd sleeve I have here though as the track is credited as a John Whitney (Instrumental) Someone has obviously taken their eye off the ball here print wise.

How-Hi-The-Li is one of my favourite Family songs, at the moment I would probably put it in second place in my affections and once again the focus of the piece is political...

And the politicians start to speak
Trying to make themselves clear
To the ones who can't diagnose
The symptoms of verbal diarrhoea

1,2,3,4 starts a laid back Ric Grech as the bass immediately gets into a prominent lead groove while Whitney's guitar chops out the rhythm behind it with Townsend's creative anchor and there are vibes, organ and saxophone harmonising behind like a Heavenly choir in the background as the laid back feel picks up pace.

Then a crashing organ and a mellow saxophone solo...

We only wanna turn the whole world on

Sings a pleading Grech; his voice now an instrument.

The bass line is superb, probably the best have ever heard and it is the bass guitar that takes us out, fading with all the instruments wailing in the distance.

And I think *wow*, a band at the top of their game; anybody that has an understanding of song-writing has to appreciate this song. It is just simply brilliant.

Second Generation Woman

The excellent How-Hi-The-Li is followed by another Ric Grech penned song which basically is a straight forward hard-hitting rocker about a woman who knows how to handle herself, *she's ahead of her time but she don't give a damn,* who maybe comes across as a femme fatale but...

She knows when her time is right
Comes to you without a fight

And you do not have to worry because…
She feeds you, loves you, let's you know she digs you
And it is Ric Grech on lead vocals as the band immediately follow Townsend's beat, Whitney's guitar singing in the background…
Ooh get in…
Then Whitney's choppy style lead guitar break, Grech singing like a love sick puppy now…
Last thing you gotta do is forcing her into loving you
And the violin crashes in towards the end with Chapman adding a ghostly strength to the chorus, Grech trying to keep up with him.

From Past Archives

There is an instant sadness about this song as Roger Chapman slips into a nostalgic mood…
Why can't we forgive, forget and be returned to harmony
A mournful, wailing harmonica, Chapman's vocals complimenting the instrument perfectly, your mood drifts along with the song then an unexpected piano and a sudden jazz-time saxophone and your mood shifts as Heavenly strings suddenly waft in the background, getting more and more intense until…
You are back to that nostalgic groove, strings heralding the end, and that jazz saxophone lifts you up again, taking you out with a good time feel…
Hoping that the song from past archives
Will soon be revived
And it is, right now as my pen makes notes on the paper.

Dim

Dim is the song that keeps appearing on that BBC Sounds of the Sixties tv programme, Chappo in a polo neck sweater, smiling and having fun as he bops along to the feel good beat. This song is a good time rocker that sees Family moving vaguely into Country territory, about going into town and having a good time…
Making my scene just groovin' around
Making what chicks I can
Drink what I like and dance what I do
Fun sounding harmonica and you can feel the excitement in Chapman's voice…
But I know there's a good time waiting for me
And then a guitar break and whistles, harmonica again…

Think I'll leap around a bit and sow my seed somewhere
Handclap*s, whoohoo*
Unexpected ending...

Processions

Then that good time beat changes once again to that feeling of nostalgic longing as a John 'Charlie' Whitney song takes us back to our childhood and those lazy hazy sun filled days at the beach...

A small boy, bucket in hand
Building castles in the sand

Beautiful piano, bass and guitar open with a wailing harmonica, Chapman's mournful vocals telling the tale of the small boy...

Thinking of his life that lies ahead

The mood wonderfully majestic as once again the instruments merge together perfectly, then the bass and a haunting saxophone and piano finish, tinkling keys only at the sad end...

The boy returned to find
That the sandcastles were washed into the sea

Has life been hard for him? Even...

The gypsy woman can't foresee the years

Another wonderful composition from Family; a beautifully nostalgic song that is guaranteed to move you emotionally. Like How-Hi-The-Li, Spanish Tide and Good News Bad News, this is one of the songs I will play to anyone who has never heard Family and if they are not moved by this great song then obviously they must not be listening properly or that they simply do not understand quality musicianship and song-writing. I do seem to remember my friend Steve's wife Jaqcui, really liking this when she heard it for the first time.

Face In The Cloud

Another Ric Grech composition and another trip back to that Summer of Love, Family trying to not let those days be forgotten. It is probably the most 'trippy' dreamy track on the album as Grech retells possibly a drink or drug induced fantasy or maybe he was just wanting to convey a feeling of wanting love...

Mountains before, reaching to Heaven
Hiding the face of a
Girl in the clouds

That eastern sound again starts the track as what sounds like a sitar with dancing drums then Grech's languid laid back sad vocals drift in and out as if it is a spaced out Lou Reed trying to get through the recording of his brilliant Berlin album.

Again there is a haunting guitar in the background, picking out the notes as Grech revisits his dream, Chapman fading in behind, echoing Grech as he comes down…

Coming down slowly from the heights of my dreams
La la la la la…

And that sitar guitar sings along with the piano.

Another song that takes you to another place, your soul drifting away, you want to see that girl in the clouds. Beautiful harmonies between Grech and Chapman and a beautiful song, my hair is long again, there are stars in my eyes, new horizons are opening up again… this is what great music can do for you.

Emotions

A stomping piano, ominous vocal harmonies open then crashing drums and strong Chapman vocals and immediately you know that the album is finishing with a powerhouse of a song. Quite apt I think as your emotions have just been on a rocking roller-coaster ride from start to finish…

Emotions you feel, around you they steal

And that then that beautiful choral harmony…

Strange, when loneliness holds you
Like a cloak that surrounds you

Chapman rasping into the main vocal lead then what sounds like a xylophone break then back to the chorus…

Chains, within and about you
Like a cage, bars to hold to
Something to remind, as the years slip behind

And then the unbelievable outro, the vocal chorus getting higher, the instruments doing that Family thing, there are even chiming bells at the end, Chapman above everything else. A fitting end then to an amazing brilliant album.

So that was my introduction to Family, I cannot remember exactly what was said by me and my mates after listening to that album in my old sitting room but it was bound to have been something like "That was just fucking unbelievable! What other albums have they made?"

And of course I went straight out and bought Music In A Doll's House when I could afford it, my fourth vinyl Long Player record and I was now a fully fledged Family fan and I have been ever since.

Review

This was the birth of progressive music then; still underground, still new, still now, still hip and still brilliant. Digging the groove still, digging the vibe. The band was not happy with the production mixes but my young ears were not aware of this at the time, the songs unique, bewitching, original and compelling. The same ingredients as Music In Doll's House but a leaner, more mature sound maybe, the sound of a band that has found it's feet, found it's groove. Like all of Family albums there is not a weak track on it, 'all killer, no filler' I believe the saying is and you always get value for money with Family. If I did have to pick out my favourite tracks then it would be How-Hi-The-Li, The Weaver's Answer, Hung Up Down, Processions, Face In The Cloud... Hell, all of them! You see what I mean.

January 1970

Children can you laugh me all your young life's meaning.
Playing as you do, I feel the truth in you.
Song For You - Roger Chapman

I saw you and you saw me.
For a moment we were free.
Will's Blues - John Weider

1

And suddenly it was 1970; the start of a new decade and the music horizon was gleaming with all sorts of creative possibilities. Glam rock and punk rock were a few short years away, music that would threaten to shake and loosen the foundations of the rock giants who would eventually succumb to a mood of musical complacency, an unexpected negative product of their own success. But I can say that this monotonous trap was something which Family did not fall into as we will see as I review how their albums evolved due to personnel changes.

At this moment I am trying to remember what other albums I had bought in 1970 - Led Zeppelin 3 and the albums by Free definitely and probably Thank Christ For The Bomb by The Groundhogs. Led Zeppelin 3 and Physical Graffiti from 1976 are probably my favourite Led Zeppelin albums, 3 has a great album cover and I have just recently bought the t-shirt, it is a mixture of psychedelic and pop art, a multitude of colourful images exploding onto a white background, the lettering looking almost like it is meant to be large balloons floating amidst the images. The music is still blues based rock but there seems to be more of a gentler vibe that was hinted at on Led Zeppelin 2 with the track Thank You.

And what a year it was for those brilliant young guys of Free, three albums released that year, Fire and Water and Highway and a live album featuring their performance at the Isle Of Wight which somehow bypassed me at the time but I do have it now and of course this was the year of their ground-breaking single All Right Now which would become a well deserved massive hit for them.

Family would also release another record in 1970, their fourth album Anyway which we will come to next, so this was a great year for a teenager who loved his music and I think that it was around this time that we had a music project to prepare at school which had to be presented to the rest of the class. I chose The Music Of Family surprise, surprise and while it was enjoyable preparing the work, it was definitely not enjoyable presenting it. I have suffered from glossophobia for most of my life, a fear of public speaking, uncomfortable making speeches, that sort of thing and I am sure that this is because I was forced to play Macbeth in the school play when I was a first year student in the senior school. Needless to say, I remember my face burning like fire as I presented the Family music project to the rest of the class. I really wish that I still had the notes for that school work but those are sadly long gone now with most of my old school exercise books which reminds me that I am still trying to find my old school haversack on which I had painted the FAMILY logo typeface, red on yellow using household gloss paint which you can almost see on the opening From Past Archives banner which is a picture of me walking off to school taken by my mother. I am sure it is in the garage somewhere, a garage that now resembles some sort of mini second-hand junk shop so finding it will be a massive task, one that unfortunately will miss the publication of this memoir but I could add it to a later edition I suppose. Fingers crossed that it is still in garage somewhere. (Damn, still haven't found it!)

But back to the music class presentation and I think that we were allowed to play four or five songs and I think that these were the five songs that were probably used that day...

The Weaver's Answer - which probably would have been played last.

How-Hi-The-Li or Processions.

Hung Up Down.

Old Songs New Songs or See Through Windows.

Drowned In Wine or Love Is A Sleeper from A Song For Me.

And even though my presentation was nervous and poor, I am sure that the content of the work was worth a grade A.

FAMILY

The A Song For Me album cover was once again black and there was no title on the front, just the FAMILY logo making its album debut in white, quite small above a large monotone brownish portrait picture of the band which is pinned against the black background. The band look relaxed, all of them smiling, Roger Chapman seated and laughing. The photograph also introduces two new band members, John Weider and Poli Palmer. Ric Grech had left during Family's debut USA tour to join the so-called supergroup Blind Faith and Jim King had left due to ever increasing erratic behaviour which was probably the result of drug over indulgence according to the rumours.

The album has a gate-fold opening and inside we have the title in red bold block capitals. The photographic montage is a bold image of the band and their instruments, with small square inserts of the different instruments they play. This is a great and powerful image of the band, Roger Chapman caught in motion hitting his tambourine and I used this spread for the banner of the Facebook Family With Roger Chapman Appreciation Society page adding **"We only wanna turn the whole world on"** from How-Hi-The-Li and along the bottom of the banner, **"Lay down easy, stars in my eyes"** from the hit single In My Own Time.

On the back of the album we find the Family logo printed onto a candle which is burning down beneath the title which is curved over it. The candle wax is slowly building as the flame burns and once again I find this a vaguely gothic image as I imagine a ghostly wind extinguishing the flame at any time. Underneath the Family candle we find two short poems by Roger Chapman and John Weider and a lengthy dedication from 'You' to 'Aslan' which includes everybody associated with Family. Nice. The album would prove to be Family's best-selling album reaching number four in the album charts.

So the question was now, what will John Weider and Poli Palmer bring to the Family table. The violin option is still there with Weider but now the saxophones have gone, replaced by Poli Palmer's flute and vibes. I knew the sound would have to change but in what way? In actual fact, the change was only subtle but I did sense that there was a much 'earthier' feel to their sound on this album which probably had a lot to do with the flute and vibes. New vibes, good vibes.

3

Roger Chapman - Vocals / Percussion/ Harmonica.
John Whitney - Guitars / Banjo / Organ.
Robert Townsend - Drums / Percussion / Harp.
John Weider - Guitars / Violin / Dobro.
John Palmer - Vibes / Piano / Flute.

Produced by Family.
Engineers, George Chkiantz, Dave Bridges, Roger Beale, Keith Harwood.
Co-ordination, Tony Gourvish.

Drowned In Wine

Family open the album A Song For Me with what was to become another great crowd pleaser live, the theme about being drowned in wine, and why not you may well ask.

A plucky instrumental guitar opens the song then the power of Roger Chapman's voice bursts in…

After the turn, you finally learn to play along
Your feelings are blind so you don't really mind if it's right or wrong
Fall in line

The music quickly gets into a stomping Family beat with a manic flute in the background then it takes lead as Chapman's voice echoes away. There is an urgency to this song, chopping guitars, singing flute, Poli Palmer's presence stamped immediately onto the sound, is that a dobro too in the background?

This is a powerful opening track with all the dynamics of the previous band with excellent new bass from Weider who was primarily not a bass player; this was a strange quirk in Family's line ups that would continue on the following albums.

And the opening intensity suddenly stops for…

Some Poor Soul

A sweet gentle beautiful acoustic guitar opens, you can hear the fingers of Charlie Whitney as they slide along the strings which is a wonderful sound and then Roger Chapman's voice is mellow until the flute floats in not as aggressive as Drowned In Wine. This is a song about nature and the importance of all living things, Roger Chapman's brilliantly descriptive lyrics observing life in a **shady wooded hollow** as the…

Moon soaked sky looks down
Giving what it has to give

A beautiful guitar break with that lovely flute then the pace picks up slightly; then you are laid back again and you start to worry about **the furry footed people…**

A crack of twigs may be poachers
I said some poor soul ain't got long to live…

Love Is A Sleeper

Then one of my favourite tracks from the album breaks away from the calmness and serenity of the previous track, a great driving thumping rocker from the start with Whitney's guitar prominent against Palmer's plonking vibes and Roger Chapman's brilliant lyrics suggest that gothic vibe again…

Love is a sleeper locked in a room
Waiting for someone to waken it

Chapman's voice floats along with the music and then the guitar and vibes break in until Chapman returns with more urgency, the tempo picking up with stop start Family rhythms...

Love is a sleeper I know
I've been so tired

The vibes, keyboards and guitars collide fighting, and the keyboards fade out to the unusual sound of the next song...

Stop For The Traffic - Through The Heart Of Me

This song sounds a bit like Observations From A Hill from the album Entertainment, there is a curious echo sound to the opening...

Stop for the traffic
Maybe I can see

And then a country beat, a bit like the song Dim as Chapman observes street life again; the music chopping and swerving, lead guitar singing and dipping then a funky acoustic break backed by a solid bass-line...

Shaking hands with people
Who are smiling desperately
Trying to win over through
Through the heart of me

An experimental fun track and one that puts a smile on your face, makes you want to immediately sing along with it until the mood changes suddenly once again...

Wheels

The tempo is languid and ominous and here again is the gothic Family, Roger Chapman at his best lyrically I think...

I'm holding a bubble no one can believe in
They look through and distort the views

The music flows with those choppy acoustic chords and background flute...

I'm holding a mirror no one wants to peek in
It's cracked they say with a wearisome moan

And there is an inner tension building...

Losing out slowly I'm trying to make good
But wheels slowly grinding
Grind slowly to mud

And then the instruments break up the beat, acoustic guitar first, fast, slow, dancing, showing Whitney's brilliance, Palmer's flute backing it until the singing vibes bring Chapman's wail into the background with a strong flute solo until you are back to the main theme, more urgency now to Chapman's vocals...

I wished for the earth, and I got me a piece
My integrity down, my soul for the lease
Vocals echoing, music still ominous, Chapman screams...
Wah yeah
Wheels keep on rolling
With the talkative guitar that fades out...

There is something dark and magical about this album and this song sums it all up for me, surely this one of Family's greatest songs.

Song For Sinking Lovers

Side two opens with yet another favourite of mine (how many times have I said that so far?) and how many times in my life have I felt like a sinking lover? And here for the first time on the album we find Weider's violin prominent in what once again sounds like a slightly 'country' style inspired song but with that Family power that is so unique.

Another slow plucking guitar opens the track with a laid back drumbeat as Roger Chapman sets the scene...

That perfume in the air is like the one she'd wear
And her hair
It always took time to repair
Then Chapman and violin crashes in, Weider's violin mournful...
Occasionally I think of things
When a cold hard bell inside me rings
Just in time I can pull the blind and shut it from my mind
The beat goes countryish again, Chapman walking on the grass...
My walk upon the grass right now it brings to pass
When she'd ask
If everything we got would last
The chorus then wailing violin, stutters back to that beat, the country violin, country guitar until the end bursts in...

Dancing wild violin, foot tapping beat, Chapman's vocals strong above it...
Shut it out...
A sad violin takes us out with the thumping drums stopping suddenly.

Hey - Let it Rock

And suddenly we're in some sort of jazz mode, *nice*, the cocktail hour maybe with a bass solo then dobro/flute behind xylophonic vibes...

Light up a candle, think about flame
Hang up the washing think about rain...
Wind up the hands on a grandfather clock
Digging the music - Hey-Let it rock...

And suddenly your sudden jazz mood stops, broken by...

The Cat And The Rat

And you are now rocking, rock and roll, fast and sweet, guitar picking the notes out Whitney style...

Well you can kick at a cat, stamp on a rat
But you bet your sweet life you won't make it

Chapman in familiar territory, crashing echoing guitars again as the pace picks up, get your blue suede shoes on buddy or your 'brothel creepers' as my girlfriend's mother used to call mine...

Well you're caught in a storm, your shoes they got worn
Insane at the rain but can't break it

And the beat is terrific, getting faster and more and more manic...

And you're glad you're alive and can shake it

Sure am.

93's ok J

This is one of those Family instrumentals that I mentioned earlier showcasing the new member's musical prowess credentials but the music is a bit more 'earthier' maybe than Summer '67 from the Entertainment album. Maybe the title came from "Take 93, that okay John?" though I do not seriously think that they did 93 takes of this song! Well it is great to finally find out from Roger that it is actually the street address of where John Whitney and John Weider lived at the time.

A beautiful guitar and violin start the song; slow at first, building, then a swaying violin melody until a clanging stop broke by chopping acoustic guitar and great rolling drums, vibes singing gently in the background, dancing. Yes, you can dance to this, lost in the rhythm, the singing guitar, the mesmeric vibes.

And suddenly there is a flute, the music has slowed down back to the main melody and the flute is now solo above that rolling Townsend drumbeat as the theme fades away... and I think that I really could listen to this all day...

But this swaying mood of mine is about to be completely shattered by the final powerhouse of a song known as…

A Song For Me

This became the Family track that ended their live performances at the time I believe and here Roger Chapman is going Poe and Shelley again.

Vibes opening like an organ from The Phantom Of The Opera, the organ rising from below, violin like spiralling waves then the electric guitar breaks in, slashing through the air with menace, Chapman's powerful vocals cutting through you like deadly vampire's teeth…

I was waiting, I was singing
I was standing patiently

And the bass is dipping and diving with Townsend's thunderous drum rhythm, Whitney's guitar fighting. This is a unique and definite Family beat, a Family rhythm building, crashing, assaulting you, Chapman asking…

Who will crack me a crooked smile
Who still climb my crooked stiles

Chapman screaming, pleading…

I was talking, I was shouting
Listen please don't turn away
Who turns deaf to what I've got to say
Who will paint my portrait grey

Keyboards and guitar take the lead as the heavy beat continues, Chapman wailing in the background…

I was crying yeah
I was stumbling, stumbling…
Over broken glass laid tracks
Following ancient portrait maps
Who's gonna tell me yeah
The paths from cracks

Then the lead guitar is prominent while the violin dances wildly around it; with Chapman echoing the vocals…

The question…

Who is gonna sing a song for me

All the instruments are manic, urgent, merging together, the violin becomes central, echoing, talking, singing, fluttering through your mind from ear to ear, low then screeching like a warning as the beat gets faster, fighting almost to find a rhythm… and then it does, almost country again, wild country style, manic heavy rock, freaking out faster and faster as the guitar breaks in. Family at full throttle as a mad piano suddenly crashes in unexpected... and you start to copy the imagined actions of a live Roger Chapman, punching the air, pointing up, smashing a tambourine until the music slows down suddenly, the violin almost panting exhausted...

Hell; that was one ending, one heavy freaking ride, my young wheels still turning long after it had finished. I remember now that I played this song to someone younger than me years later, someone who was a massive Eric Clapton fan and someone who had not been too impressed by Roger Chapman's solo work although he did admit that he had only heard one or two songs, not enough really to make judgement and A Song For Me simply blew him away, Whitney's riff work making a big impression on him and these day's he acknowledges how good and underrated Family were. I think with this track he suddenly understood what Family were about, where Chapman had come from, that there was a 'guitar' sound but it was not the be all and end all of their music, that there were a lot of intricate and complicated ingredients within it that contributed to the unique and original sound.

Review

Inevitably, two new members in any band will mean a change in style and sound and A Song For Me is representational of Poli Palmer's and John Weider's creative contribution to the album. There does seem to be a slight difference in the sound but remember that these are still Chapman and Whitney compositions, the exception being the Whitney and Weider instrumental 93's okJ and Weider is also credited on the violin driven title track.

Now the Family sound has vibes and prominent flute but there is still violin which is definitely more manic on certain tracks. And the power and dynamics of Family are still evident as we see in Drowned In Wine, Love Is A Sleeper, Wheels and the climatic A Song For Me

New additions to a band can be a worry for established band members and fans alike, but it was great to realise that Poli Palmer and John Weider were valuable additions, highly talented musicians who would fit perfectly into the Family sound and once again the next album was now something to really look forward to and nine months later Family would give birth to Anyway.

A Song For Me would prove to be Family's best selling album at the time reaching number 4 in the UK charts... which sort of makes me wonder what the their overall best-selling album really is, fifty years later on? I can only think that Roger Chapman would know the answer to that.

The last quote on the back cover of the album sleeve says it all, "See you tomorrow Tom, everybody have a good time."

And we did.

ANYWAY

November 1970

A mist comes o'er the shore, from out the sea's embrace,
The sun just going down the red without a face

1

1970 turned out to be very productive and very successful for Family with the release of their second album that year in November and the Strange Band single which proved to be a success in the charts for The Weaver's Answer which reached number 11 in the charts. Family were truly on the rock map now and a major draw live playing all the big venues and festivals. I remember reading, and I really wish that I could remember where and when, that Jimi Hendrix would have in his festival contract that he would not follow Family live, which has to be because they were that that good live which really is high praise indeed.

It has been said that the band were a bit unhappy with the live side and that it was always a regret of theirs that they never released a decent live album by their standards but I have to say that the live side more than lived up to my expectations as we shall see later on.

In 1970, I was fifteen years of age and I think I had not yet seen any bands live and now I wish I still had my old scrapbook with my concert tickets and music press cuttings about my favourite bands stuck in it but unfortunately it vanished in the mists of time probably on my Dad's coal fire like my now valuable comic collection. It would not be until 1971 when I would see Family live and I think that the first band that I ever saw live was Jethro Tull at the Sunderland Empire. I must have seen Free there too because I remember the support act Amazing Blondel. I am trying now to think of all the bands I have seen live over the years...

Family

Streetwalkers with Chapman / Whitney

Roger Chapman and the Shortlist
Jethro Tull
Free
Roxy Music
Bryan Ferry solo
The Groundhogs
Captain Beefheart and the Magic Band
Vinegar Joe with Elkie Brooks and Robert Palmer
Steeleye Span
John Cale with Chris Spedding
Siouxsie and the Banshees
The Stranglers
Eddie and the Hot Rods
The Pretenders
KT Tunstall
New Order
Simple Minds
John Martyn
Elbow

And last but not least because I hope to see many more live concerts in whatever time I have left; Mr. Brian Eno - The Relationship Between Guerrilla Warfare And Modern Music which was an early lecture by him at Canterbury College of Architecture. As a young graphic art student I found this lecture both magical and enlightening and I vividly remember the multiple still slides of the small airliner, distant in the grey sky moving slowly across the lecture screen. Here was Eno in cerebral mode and I did take notes in a small notebook which once again, I have lost and I wish I still had. That night, Eno walked right past me in the lecture hall, *now why did I not stop him and ask him to sign that notebook?* I keep asking myself, I definitely would not have lost it if he had. Sometimes you feel that you could just kick yourself, don't you when you think about the mistakes of the past.

Recently, out of the blue because I had made a comment on a Jethro Tull Facebook page about Tull being my first concert, I was asked to write down and submit my memories of that Sunderland Empire Jethro Tull concert for a Jethro Tull book about fan's memories. I now know that my short memoir of that concert will be included in the excellent Lend Me Your Ears by Richard Houghton because the organisers thought that my review was fabulous and I have since been asked for a photograph of myself at that age which is promising and something to definitely look forward to. I thought that it would be cool to include this memoir here as Jethro Tull is one of my favourite bands still.

The picture of me used in Jethro Tull Lend Me Your Ears book,
(a bit older here though than what I was at the Tull concert I have to say.)

JETHRO TULL
Sunderland Empire 20/03/1971
A Concert Memory
by
RICHARDVALANGA

When you get to my age, a memory from 1971 can be an elusive beast, you have to try and conjure it up as best you can and simply hope that it is close to being accurate. But these days there is the web checking facility of the All Knowing Mighty Google to help you out and that is a Godsend.

Jethro Tull at the Sunderland Empire 20th March 1971 and I was there as a star struck teenager aged fifteen. My 2021 memory tried to fool me though, it was not the Amazing Blondel that were supporting Jethro Tull, it was in fact the electric folk rock band Steeleye Span and now I realise that I would seen Amazing Blondel with Free. For some reason, Blondel and Tull had merged together in my mind, maybe it was because there was possibly a sort of similarity to both bands in certain aspects both musically and visually although I have to state that Amazing Blondel were certainly not as electric and as powerful as Jethro Tull.

Jethro Tull played two concerts at the Empire that day and I think it would have been the early show that I attended considering my age. I do not recall owning a Jethro Tull album at that time as my vinyl collection was in it's infancy but I was aware of the unique brilliance of the singles and of the tv performances featuring the visually striking and energetic Ian Anderson.

And this is a vivid memory of the concert, the singer of Jethro Tull, the iconic stance of playing the flute, standing on one leg, the half ragged brown check antique looking jacket and the amazing frizzed out flowing hair that sometimes looked like it had a life of it's own. Then Ian strutting across the stage; waving his flute about like the wand of some wild manic magician from the medieval ages trying to draw us all into his spell.

The rest of the band were Martin Barre on guitar, Clive Bunker on drums, John Evan on keyboards and Jeffrey Hammond-Hammond on bass and were not quite as visual as their curious enigmatic front man but they were brilliant musicians at the top of their game, the album Aqualung was only one day old and confirmed this. The set list was probably the following - Nothing Is Easy, Aqualung, Hymn 43, My God, Cross-Eyed Mary, With You There to Help Me, By Kind Permission Of; Sossity: You're a Woman; Reasons for Waiting; Wind Up; Guitar solo, Locomotive Breath; Hard-Headed English General; Wind Up (reprise)

I do remember leaving the Empire thinking *Wow; I've just seen one of the world's greatest rock bands!* I know for a fact that the next day I bought Aqualung and I have a vivid memory of playing the record in my bedroom, the windows wide open just to give the neighbours a slice of brilliant rock. The next album for me would be the excellent Stand Up and from that moment on I was an avid fan and have remained so to this day and I now have a large collection of all things Jethro Tull, cd and dvd in my music library. Those now distant, sometimes hazy faraway days were Tulltastic (wonder if Alan Fluff Freeman ever said that?) and I am so glad that I was there when The Golden Age Of Rock Music was just beginning.

Richard Valanga
27/06/2021.

What an introduction to live music then! Tull were superb, showing why they were on the verge of international stardom, which their excellent album Aqualung would secure for them. Later in 1971, I would see Family for the first time; these were great days for a young music fan. I think it was in 1971 that me and my friends from school started going to the Locarno Ballroom or The Mecca as it was locally known, as this was where the music of all our favourite bands would be played on a Thursday and Sunday night. These were very cool times for a young 'Hairey' (not exactly a peace loving Hippy, Haireys could be rough fighters as sometimes you did have to defend yourself in Sunderland) and The Mecca was the place to be if you wanted to hear underground, progressive rock music. I remember the colourful clothes and man how those young hippy chicks sparkle now in my mind, I remember back combing the sides of my long hair in a vain attempt to look like Paul Kossoff and I remember that strange new joss stick smell and wondering what those older guys were smoking? I remember the hippy 'idiot' dancers freaking out on the dance floor; I remember walking round and round the Mecca, upstairs and downstairs, looking at all the beautiful girls and I did get a girlfriend there for a short while there but nothing came of it, we were both very shy and young and just cuddled in the dim light of the dark corners of the hall. Most of all though, I remember my mind being blown away by all the great music. If I had the money, it would be great to re-open a venue like that and play all that wonderful music from those great magical days, The New Mecca sounds good to me, all I have to do now is win the Lottery.

Actually, I now remember that there was a sort of re-union for Mecca 'veterans' a few years ago at the Sinatra's pub club in Sunderland which I went to. Geoff Docherty, who became *the* major promoter of great bands in Sunderland and the North East, was there and I have to say that the most played band that night was Family. Geoff was a doorman for The Bay Hotel in Whitburn and was given a chance to promote a major up-coming band there which turned out to be Family, if they had bombed that night then so would have his promoting career as he recalls in his book A Promoter's Tale. Of course Family were brilliant and a great success for Geoff, which led to him booking more bands and eventually becoming the biggest promoter in the North East. I take my Family hat off to you Geoff and thanks for the memories.

One of my Family hats and my Charlie Whitney t-shirt.

The Bay Hotel, Whitburn.

Actually, as I edit this section, I now remember that I wrote about Family's first concert at The Bay Hotel in my paranormal novel Complex Reality, a concert that I obviously had to imagine and I think it would be interesting to include it here. In the story, one the main characters accidentally finds himself at this concert...

"I would get yourself there quickly mate before that cold of yours gets any worse, you do not look too well," he said then the family continued on their walk along the beach... and I was grateful that the dark conscious did not consume me. The man had only tried to be helpful.

Following his advice, I ascended the multitude of winding steps that took me up the cliff and onto the road back towards Seaburn and within half an hour I was at the Bay Hotel. The hotel was a large building that was not far from the main road. It was painted white and its style of architecture was thirties art déco. I think it would have looked perfectly at home in any Hollywood movie of the time.

The hotel had a vast function hall and this night it looked as if it was going to be busy. Outside of the function door there was a large crowd waiting to be let in. I noticed that the crowd was mainly made up of young people, dressed not unlike myself and many of the men had long hair. There was also a large element of what the press was now calling 'hippies' with their afghan coats and flared jeans. I quickly realised that this was a rock concert and this intrigued me, *whoever was playing must be quite popular* I thought. *Could it be the Beatles or the Rolling Stones?* I thought. No, both were far too big now but I did listen to the radio and knew that the new 'underground' rock scene was beginning to take the music industry by storm.

As I neared the front door I noticed a large poster for the band that was playing - THE FAMILY, and underneath was a picture of a large doll on a child's tricycle. Whatever this symbolised I had no idea but the poster was advertising the band's debut album called *Music In A Doll's House*. Again, I was intrigued, and after all it was a Friday night and a young man like me should be out enjoying himself. I stepped towards the door...

"No way, mate, you need to take your place in the queue."

A smart, casually dressed man was standing in front of me and I could tell by the look on his face that he meant business.

"I think you can let them in now Geoff, let's get your show on the road" somebody called from behind him and I stepped aside.

The thirst was still raging though and I needed a drink fast, I could not wait till the crowd was inside ahead of me and the bar was full. I walked to the side of the hotel and when I was sure that nobody could see me, I disappeared. Walking invisibly back to the entrance, I breezed inside and into a toilet cubicle where I reappeared. I had thought about staying unseen all night but there was no need, it would have only meant that people would have kept bumping into me... and I think it is easier to get served when the barman can actually see you!

My first port of call then was the bar where I purchased three pints of McEwans best scotch and drank them all in one go.

"Hey, take it easy my friend, the band's not on for another hour or so. You do want to see them, don't you?" said the big, burly barman who was obviously worried by this and I saw him nod to another stout man who was obviously one of the concert 'bouncers.' I had to think of a quick retort.

"Just finished my weekend shift and it was thirsty work," I said and this seemed to satisfy him, I noticed that he shook his head slightly to the watching hard man at the side of the bar.

I bought another beer and I could feel that my red eyes had reverted back their natural green colour. As I began to walk away from the bar, I noticed that an attractive young girl with long black hair had been watching me, obviously intrigued by my apparent insatiable thirst.

As I looked at her she became quite shy and turned to talk with her friend. She was wearing a thin denim jacket that covered a white t-shirt that was adorned with large blue stars. Her tight blue jeans were held up with a thick brown belt and the bottom of her jeans was flared like so many of the people in the concert hall. She seemed to be wearing a lot of make-up but I found this girl quite stunning and attractive.

I decided to sit at a side table near the front of the stage, take my time with my new drink and wait and see what this mysterious Family were like.

I think it was about 8.30 pm when some of the band shambled quite unceremoniously onto the stage. The hall was completely full by then and the people standing at the front of the stage were obviously fans who began to clap and chant the name Chapman. The rest of the audience seemed quite indifferent though - this was obviously a new band they had come to check out.

The Chapman in question was the lead singer and as the band kicked off with a strong groove to How Many More Years, the vocalist sauntered onto the stage, tambourine in hand. He was very tall and thin but with a lithe, muscular frame and as soon as he started singing an excited buzz consumed the room. The audience were enthralled and the faithful fans that knew the band started dancing (freaking out, I seem to remember it being called) immediately. I had never been to a rock concert before and I was caught up in the excitement and was amazed by the complete abandonment of the 'loon' dancers at the front who were obviously trying to mimic the manic movements of the enigmatic singer... and what a voice this man had, I had never heard anything so unique or powerful.

The band continued with a few more blues classics before announcing that they were going to play tracks from their debut album. This brought rapturous applause from the knowing fans and the band launched into a soft, moody song called The Breeze and this time it was the lyrics that caught my attention.

About how nobody can see the breeze.

Nobody knows what it is.

Who it is.

I related to these words instantly... I could be that breeze.

The music was like no other I had ever heard and the words reached out and instantly struck a chord deep within me. They played a heavy, doom laden song called Voyage next and I sensed that the song was about death's dark journey. A journey I was all too aware of now.

A song called Me My Friend caught my attention also.

About wanting to sail to the stars.

Your whole body and mind transported there.

To a new world of dreams.

These words seemed to have been written for me - from that moment on I knew that I would collect songs that referenced my love of Astronomy, *Music In A Doll's House* was a must buy then.

The concert was a huge success, enjoyed by the whole audience that showed their appreciation vocally. The band did many encores which saw the magnificent Mr. Chapman smashing tambourines and swinging like Tarzan on speed from the tall palm trees at the side of the stage.

As the hall lights came up, I made my way with the jubilant crowd through the exit doors into a cold but dry night. Most of the people drifted slowly off in various directions but some formed small groups and talked about the great band they had just seen. These groups of people were smiling and laughing, still dancing even and I suspected that it was not just the music that had raised their spirits this icy winter's night.

One group however, did not look happy. Two girls and three young men seemed to be arguing on the corner of the street directly opposite the calm, dark sea. One of the girls was Miss Blue Star, the girl that had looked so intrigued about me at the bar... and she seemed to be concerned and troubled.

I have mentioned the music of my favourite bands in my novels over the years, a bit like Stephen King mentions music in most of his novels as a device to instil an immediate atmosphere and I guess when I have mentioned Family, it is just my way of keeping the Family Flame burning.

2

One thing you can definitely say about Family is that they were always innovative and the album Anyway was no exception. The album cover is the artwork, 'Mortars with Exploding Projectiles' by Leonardo da Vinci. Had that ever been done before, a famous artwork being used for the cover of an LP? The only one's I can think of at the moment at that particular time are the Velvet Underground's banana album cover by Andy Warhol and the Beatle's Sgt. Peppers album cover by Peter Blake which are more contemporary modern artworks and I guess that I am talking about famous artworks by a famous classical artist from history here.

The other unique innovation is that side one of Anyway is live, recorded at Fairfields Hall, London, new songs released live before any studio versions with the exception of the track Strange Band which had been released as a single of course. Surely this had never been done before? A gamble you might think but this was Family, they always did things their way, they never did the safe and the expected.

I do not remember buying the album, it might have been bought again for me by my mother after her 6 till 2 nursing shift. I do remember looking at the cover though in the sitting room, my father sitting opposite who seemed to be very impressed by the Leonardo da Vinci cover.

The gate-fold cover is inserted into a slightly mottled transparent sleeve with a flap top which has the words **FAMILY. ANYWAY**… in a golden new type-style that was different to the now famous one on A Song For Me. Why they did not use this FAMILY logo is a slight mystery to me being an advertising art director and graphic designer as they had used it on the successful single Strange Band. At the moment I do not know what the typeface is but it is quite distinguishable and seems to suit the artwork it is superimposed onto perfectly.

The inside of the album cover is a lovely golden orange and it includes the lyrics to all the songs. I always think that a couple of live images of the band from the recorded concert should have been added to this inside cover but the album cover is definitely a unique work of art and design by Hamish & Gustav, the mortar symbolising Family surely and the exploding projectiles their music.

When the music started though, I do not think that my father was too impressed, leaving the room with a wry grin on his face, his excuse being that it was time for him to get ready to go to the club but it was not really his type of music and instantly Family were in a loud and heavy rocking mode with the opening track.

So here I was, about to hear Family live for the first time and boy was my mind about to be blown away. I can still feel that youthful excitement as I look at the cover and the words to the first song…

What is the point, you'll never win
We're up at your throats before you begin

3

Roger Chapman - Vocals / Percussion / Harmonica.
John Whitney - Guitar / Bass / Banjo / Organ.
Robert Townsend - Drums / Percussion.
John Weider - Guitars / Violin / Electric Piano.
John Palmer - Vibes / Piano / Flute / Percussion.

Produced by Family.
Engineers, George Chkiantz and Steve, Chris, Anton, Skinhead Dave, Jock and Topper.

Good News Bad News

My favourite three songs by Family are Spanish Tide, How-Hi-The-Li and Good News Bad News which I think I have already stated and the 'Holy Grail' for me concerning Family is to hear a studio version of Good News Bad News which has never surfaced anywhere to my knowledge at this moment in time. C'mon Chappo, there must be at least a studio rehearsal recording of the song somewhere? I really would love to hear it and I bet a million other Family fans would also.

   This is a song about the down-trodden maybe, about not letting life and the bastards grind you down, about change being a good thing possibly. Anyway reached number 7 in the charts which meant three brilliant top ten albums on the trot for Family and as soon as this record starts, you realise that it is truly well deserved.

Tuning, vibes, bass note…

Then chopping Whitney guitar getting louder, *Yeah* in the background, Chapman screaming ***Aaahh*** then in come the crashing drums…

What is the point… Vibes behind…

Closing their ears… Powerhouse vocals then quietly…

Turning your head away from the crowd

Then that power repeated with Whitney's vicious guitar, smashing drums, Chapman screaming until the band hit a groove with Palmer's vibes prominent backed by perfectly pitched guitar and a great dancing bass line by Weider, foot stomping along with Palmer's tune.

Then the tension builds again with that guitar intro into a fierce Whitney guitar break, expressive, drums still crashing around, rolling to Whitney's rocking rhythm, bass biting in the background. Whitney shows his strength here as a great lead guitarist and then the music dips into that crashing riff, Chapman howling in the background…

Then it goes quiet again…

Why change the rules, say those at the top

Then the power of Chapman's vocals repeat…

Hey, yeaah

Vicious drums chopping with menace, the guitar riff biting until…

Stop.

And the crowd go wild…

"Thank you… thank you very much

Er, this is a song called Willow Tree…"

Willow Tree

I remember reading or listening to an interview somewhere in which Roger Chapman sort of dismissed Willow Tree briefly for some reason as if he were slightly embarrassed by the song, as if it belonged to another era maybe? Well, I have to say that I must have interpreted this wrong as the recent feedback by Roger is that he loved the song which is really great to know. I think Willow Tree is great, a song which harks back to that laid back hippy feel, with descriptive magical surreal lyrics and what I like about Anyway is that it tells you what each member is playing on each track.

Here we have an acoustic sounding song with Charlie Whitney on bass guitar, Poli Palmer on piano and John Weider on violin. A song about the loss of a lover with the metaphor being the willow tree which has a beautiful opening with piano and bass...

Willow tree wooden, were you once a woman

Then the violin floats in, then a plucking break, Chapman singing and floating above the music. Then crashing, quick tempo piano with drums rattling, violin soaring sounding almost horn-like until the violin dances and the band get into a groove until that lonely bass, piano and haunting violin creep in then that slow pizzicato as the music fades away with piano.

Holding The Compass

"Ah, here's a new song, wrote on the bus, good job..." (I think)

Destined to become a Family favourite, I always felt that this was an optimistic song, that if you chose the wrong path in life, there was always a way to get back home; that you will never get lost holding the right compass...

Many a time I'll point to a sign, which way to go

An amplified acoustic opening by Weider and Whitney with a choppy dancing, knee tapping rhythm...

Whoever you are, just pick out a star
To shine your light

There is a great good time feel to this song and you feel like smiling as you sail along with it and it's funky rhythm with percussion chopping, dipping and diving, guitars echoing acoustically, Chapman coming in belting out the words...

Computer brain could guide a train along its path

The tempo picking up, Chapman rolling along with the pulsating sound and again you want to dance along with him.

Strange Band

Here you are hit with instant vivid imagery, a sudden snapshot of a blind man and his dog on the road and a couple in a car, uncomfortable together while a ghostly figure sits in the shade of a tree on a hill. It is film noir novella fiction that makes you want to know what happens to these odd characters next.

A bit of on-stage banter about the song being "a new song and grooving around the kings Road..."

"Okay bandy..." (I think)

A manic high pitched violin opens then crashing guitar and drums, violin fighting the intrusion, vibes immediate, Chapman's vocals ferocious...

Dog and his master, took out together
Heading due west, away from the east
Walking the road, leading a blind man
Staff in his hand, and a dog that could see
Strange looking band were we

The beat urgent then a soaring violin break until the guitar breaks in with that chopping Whitney style rhythm until Chapman belts out the vocals, the pace getting crazy, you can hear Chapman destroying his tambourine, Palmer's vibes feverish until that stop start rhythm kicks in, violin floating, drums crashing again then thumping out the end. The crowd go wild again, wanting more.

And I want more and I wish that Anyway had been a double album with live versions of all the new studio songs and studio versions of all the new live songs. I would have definitely paid the extra money... and also I have to ask, where is the rest of the Fairfields Hall concert? That could have been an album surely that could have been released later because the band were on fire that night, like all nights I have to say, Family always gave 100% and more.

The first side of Anyway displays the explosive power that was Family live, the unique dynamics of their music, the versatility and diverse elements of their sound, four live songs that gave me an immediate craving to see them live and I suppose anybody else who had listened to this album. So how would the studio side follow that? Easy, three great songs and another intriguing instrumental.

Part Of The Load

Part Of The Load was composed by Roger Chapman and Charlie Whitney while the band was on tour in America and you can hear it in the sound of the song, feel it in the lyrics as Roger Chapman writes about life on the road, the vastness of the States compared to the UK and why you never ask your lady to wait. This is a song that is another Family favourite, a song that they loved to play live, to extend and improvise in that unique Family manner, another powerhouse in the Family cannon.

The song starts with a clear solo bass line that seems to be asking a question, a question that is immediately answered by a stuttering drumbeat...

Then vibes and Chapman's vocals crash in...

Got here this morning, leaving on Saturday

Whitney's guitar amazingly sounds like a long haulage truck somehow as the music and Chapman's vocals merge, piano, truck-guitar hitting a funky beat, truck-horn sound to the guitar, Chapman's hands clapping along with a piano solo...

Down the road, down the road, hey...

Chappo repeats **Woah, ahaah**

Chapman's vocals are so great on this track, the Townsend's drumbeat just right as Chapman echoes in the background while the band get back to that driving beat, piano plonking, sound of the motorway, car horns and brakes screeching, then Whitney's eerie night sounding guitar solo fades...

Anyway

A mist comes o'er the shore from out of the sea's embrace

Here we have the title track and I find this a very mystical and mysterious song, one for imaginative lazy dreamers perhaps. Beautifully descriptive as two lovers walk in the moonlight, the man has given his coat to keep his lady warm, holding her tight in the evening glade.

A booming drumbeat opens the song, castanets click and echo, guitar to Chapman's dreamlike vocals. The music floats but the guitars are frantic in the background...

The snow becomes a mirror for the northern star

There you are

Echo drums like kettle drums solo with a thumping bass, vibes beginning to almost sound a warning in the background but the lovers are safe...

A willow spreads its limbs to make a lover's shade

Anyway

Chapman's voice harmonious as an instrument as the vibes echo and buzz into...

Normans

I seem to remember that Normans was possibly a café where Family would hang out occasionally and it has also been said that Normans is band slang for a certain type of guy that would hang around at the time.

This instrumental has a sort of funky jazz feel to it. The drums stomp us into a violin piano groove, both fighting against each other as the song drives along until a quiet piano interlude... then back to the main rhythm, violin so expressive until a lonely sounding flute takes the lead.

Then the main theme crashes back in, piano and violin together still duelling, then Chapman's background vocals are prominent, soft and gentle, harmonising again until the violin again takes centre stage.

Lives And Ladies

Here we find Roger Chapman in a nostalgic political mood, Lives And Ladies is an anti-war song about mother's and fathers who worry about their sons caught up in some conflict, about the soldiers themselves, who are not quite sure what they are fighting for. Then people from Chapman's home town possibly appear in the song, his friends who are salesmen and tailors who just love their wives and their children, they do not want the horror of war, they do not need war so please do not go pulling your switches or pressing your buttons...

A laid back opening with drums and piano...

People that you send to war, they don't know what they're fighting for

Chapman's voice is soft, the guitar is mournful. A slow song initially but the tempo builds with that familiar Family dynamic, a slow funky beat as Chapman's anger and cynicism builds...

I hope you're satisfied

Then Whitney's lonely guitar comes in, sounding sad then getting louder, a lonely piano accompanies it and the break gets longer, more and more expressive, just right until the main theme comes back in, Chapman singing about the friends he knows in Leicester...

He loves his lady and baby
And he's sure that you love yours
So don't go pulling your switches
We don't need your wars

Repeated as the guitar goes fuzzy, the frantic piano fading; hands clapping as the music disappears; the beat still going strong...

Review

The unusual half live, half studio hybrid is a brilliant success for me but I have stated earlier that a double album would have been perfect, a big statement about what Family were at the time. Once again the song-writing is superb and the dynamics of the Family Power is still there and even more evident because of the live tracks as displayed on Good News Bad News and Strange Band.

Things were going to change on the music horizon though but I feel Family were still trying to hold onto that 'Summer of Love' vibe with songs like Willow Tree and the title track Anyway. Family did try to keep that sixties vibe going on the next two albums but there was a more modern contemporary feel to it... by the final album It's Only A Movie though, that 'hippy' vibe had just about disappeared, replaced by a switch in mood that suggested an Americana feel to Family's music, one that would be carried over onto the excellent Chapman / Whitney album called Streetwalkers.

And I do have to say here that the Streetwalkers album cover remains my favourite cover, mainly because of nostalgic reasons I guess but also I love the sixties 'The Avengers' and 'The Prisoner' tv series vibe it somehow evokes.

March 1971

Old songs new songs, keep on singing

1

1971 brought the much loved Old Songs New Songs compilation album for the amazingly low price of only £1.49p, low priced because Family knew that there were no new songs on it. It was a project that I think the guys in Family wanted to do though as the songs were remixed re-dubbed and produced by Family.

I think the album is loved, especially by me, because it included singles and tracks that were not on previous albums - Today, Good Friend Of Mine, Hometown and No Mule's Fool. The other tracks are Hung Up Down, Observations From A Hill, Drowned In Wine, Peace Of Mind, The Cat And The Rat, See through Windows and finally The Weaver's Answer. As I have hinted at, it was probably the tracks from Entertainment that probably inspired this album, tracks that the band were not happy about, having been mixed in their absence. And I do think that the songs are better, much stronger and clearer I feel, especially when listened to with earphones.

2

Once again we have an intriguing album design by Stuart Weston and even though I suspect that there was probably not much of a budget with Old Songs New Songs, he has come up with something that is simplistic but effective and memorable.

The front cover is black and white with great pictures of the band in action across the top which has their names underneath. The bold title typography is spit in two with OLD SONGS in a decorative vaudeville/circus style typeface and underneath NEW SONGS in a plain modern type style. Underneath the large title is the track listening and album information normally found on the back of the album which also gives song credits to departed members Ric Grech and Jim King. There is a reason why this information is on the front of this single sleeve though and that is because the back of the album cover is a complete reverse negative of the front cover.

At the bottom of the cover, in what seems like a sign-like border is the old familiar FAMILY style logo which was sadly not to grace another Family album cover. Was this a branding mistake by the individual album designers and also maybe the band? I personally think that it was possibly, like I think they should have kept the CHAPMAN / WHITNEY song-writing brand instead of going for the Streetwalkers band name. However, I do have to state here that the final three albums were still outstanding award winning works of art and design as we shall see further on.

So let me now discuss the four non-album tracks on Old Songs New Songs.

3

Re-mixed, re-dubbed and produced by Family.

Engineer, George Chkiantz.

Co-ordination, Tony Gourvish.

Today

I love this song but I have to say that I think it was an unusual selection for a single which was released in April 1970, the B-side being the up tempo fun track Song For Lots. Today is a slow song as we shall see and some would agree I am sure that the livelier Song For Lots, a song about Lots Road where Family used to live, should maybe have been the A-side even though it is not the better song of the two. Unfortunately, I have to say here that I think the selection of singles throughout Family's career may have on occasion, let them down somewhat, with the exception of the hits of course. An example of another poor choice of single that immediately springs to mind; is the song Boom Bang from their last album It's Only A Movie. Boom Bang is a tremendous brilliant song that I really love, a song that I still find hard to define but I think it was not hit single material especially with it's at times, airwave unfriendly lyrics.

Back to Today though, which is a song that seems to be about being optimistic about the troubles and strife's of life but that good time feeling is there, you just have to reach out because it is near you...

It could be near you
It should be clear too

If you change your ways, bend your ways, keep on trying, then things will be alright, even though there will be tears along the way.

But do it today...

Today has a sad sounding start, acoustic guitar and electric backing; then Chapman opens, almost whispering the words...

One thing
is showing
We know
it's growing
Bend your way
Today

The music crying behind him, still slow, building slightly as Chapman's voice rises...

Today, today...

Vibes and slide guitar continue the main theme and rhythm then...

We'll keep on trying
We'll keep on crying

Cymbals float behind the guitar that rises then an acoustic guitar crashes in, Chapman's percussive tambourine shaking, bongos, the guitar wailing as Chapman repeats ***Today*** in a beautiful sublime melody, the guitar getting higher then suddenly down again and then fading with a spiralling sound.

Hometown

Hometown is the B-side to the single Second Generation Woman and a great inclusion on Old Songs New Songs. It is a song about going back to your home town and noticing the changes that have been made, some not so good.

Grass is gone
There's only concrete
to walk upon

Roger Chapman is in astute observation mode again. I feel that this is a song about Roger returning home after a lengthy absence possibly, something that has happened to most of us probably.

I remember returning to Sunderland after my college years in London...

How strange
People thinking
that I've changed
But as it happens
I'm just the same
It's just the cut of clothes
I wear...

Art college days.

And yes, I did feel that people thought that I had changed because I was wearing Brylcreem in my hair and a motorbike jacket and straight jeans instead of flared jeans. I was now in a retro rock and roll Americana groove, ahead of the fashion game at the time.

Strange isn't it, how people still judge you by the clothes you wear?

A beautiful guitar opening with tabla style drums and xylophone / vibraphone prominent behind Chapman's soft reflective vocals that as he thinks about the changes to his home town drift into the chorus...

Hometown, everything has been changed around
Building so high, can't even spy
The sun going down

The melodic nostalgia continues and now the violin is prominent, gliding along, really enforcing the sad reflective mood to the song, *Oah oooh* Chapman harmonise then fades.

No Mule's Fool

You will find that the song No Mule's Fool is at the top of their favourite list for a lot of Family people. A relatively simple song by Family's standards but simplicity can be so effective if executed correctly and Family achieve this here, another sign of their genius. The song was released as a single during October 1969, the B-side being the emotive Good friend Of Mine. Basically No Mule's Fool is a song about taking life easy, told through the eyes of a guy and his old mule. The setting could be some rural village or even an old American western town but the message is the same; chill out and relax.

Spend your lazy days and ways just turning on

And as I sit here in my garden, in the heat of the sun summer 2021, this is what I seem to be doing as I start to listen to the song...

We make our own rules and it's cool

Gentle acoustic guitar strumming, slow drums as the guitar picks out the tune then Chapman opens...

A dusty day in this old town

And the story unfolds of the lazy traveller, the guitar and violin complimenting the lyrics as we drift along in the haze of the sunny day painted so perfectly by Chapman.

Then the tempo suddenly picks up, the violin is more urgent, louder as it bursts into a spontaneous faster riff, guitar plucking, foot tapping...

My old mule, nobody's fool

Good Friend Of Mine

It is great to find out that this is a song by Roger to Ric Grech, they had been pals since the X-Citers long before Family. I feel that this song is about the lasting friendship of two old school friends, one of which has been lucky enough to get an education, the other has been through financially lean times, having been married and on the breadline. But through it all they have remained good friends and maybe the message of the story is that money and wealth are not everything, the friendship of an old friend is far more important. I know this to be true because my lifelong friend Steve Nanson was there for me in the aftermath of the death of my dear son Carl and I will forever be grateful to him. I lost a good friend of mine Mick Averre a few years ago and this memoir is dedicated to both him and Steve and also of course, my son's Carl and James who both did genuinely like the music of Family and Roger Chapman, having seen Roger live on a few occasions with me. I love the photograph of Mick on the dedication page of this memoir; it looks like it almost belongs on the back of Entertainment with the rest of the band which is quite apt because it was because of Mick that I first heard Entertainment. So Good Friend Of Mine always makes me think of Mick and Steve, God bless you both my dear friends.

A quiet distant piano starts slowly, a lonely bass then Chapman begins the story until hard hitting drums and guitar punctuate the words, vibes floating in the background that take the lead. Then Chapman's vocal power increases...

Said I've worked like a slave till my dad died, my mother and me went crying... Chapman really belting the words out now with what sounds like a low saxophone, wrestling together, wringing out the emotions...

You're still a good friend of mine

One of my favourite badges from those Fearless times.

Family portrait to celebrate their new album.
Back – Charlie Whitney, John Weider, Roger Chapman.
Front – Poli Palmer with drink, beautiful guest, Rob Townsend with horn.
Picture courtesy of Roger Chapman.

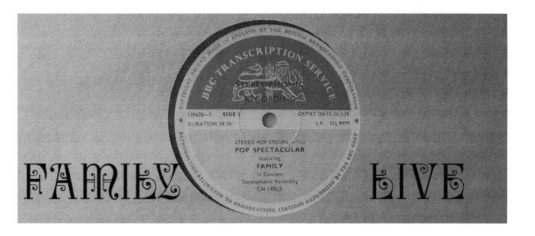

1971

"This is John Peel from the BBC in London and this is another one of our concert programmes and this week we have one of the best bands that we have in Great Britain and they are Family!"

1

School and SAFC Boys days, great memories, great times.

On the 13th November 1971, I finally got to see Family live at the Newcastle City Hall. I was sixteen, still at school and still playing for Sunderland Boys Football Team. The main supporting act was a band from America who were actually called America and who went on to become quite big in the States and I do seem to remember that me and my friends were impressed by their song Horse With No Name which I bought as a single and which went on to be a massive hit for them, both here and back in the States.

I do have to state quite clearly though that my memory of seeing Family live is somewhat hazy these days, a young boy with two many bottles of Newcastle Brown Ale is not a good combination for the memory cells especially fifty years later. However, there are visual snapshots in my mind that are still there thankfully.

I went to the City Hall with my friends and our girlfriends, a young gang from Sunderland, all the way to Newcastle and we managed to get served under-age in the nearest pub to the venue, the name of which eludes me now. I was probably wearing my first Family t-shirt, only the stencil image of Roger Chapman singing has survived the years which you can see below...

The t-shirt was actually red not pink but obviously the red colour has faded dramatically over the years. I must have bought the shirt from an advertisement in either, the Sounds, the New Musical Express or the Melody Maker, music magazines which I bought every week without fail. I saved the image of Roger Chapman purely because I did not have the heart to throw it out with the remains of the shirt, I think I did consider sewing it onto a new shirt but I never got round to it but now I have an idea, my sister Dot has a sewing machine I think...

Actually, thinking about sewing, I remember sewing FAMILY onto the back of a Levi denim shirt using bits of denim from old jeans and I have to say that it was really impressive and that I was really surprised by my sewing skills, sadly though, an irate stupid girlfriend tore it up some years later in a fit of anger after yet another argument, some people know how to hurt, don't they. Another great sewing feat of mine was making the bottom of my jeans into flares from the knee just like the jeans of Paul Rodgers of Free, they were really cool I seem to remember and I remember people asking me where I had bought them. This was all hand sewing and I do remember taking ages with both the shirt and the jeans but it was a labour of love.

Back to the Newcastle City Hall though and the Family set would have included new songs from the album Fearless which was released in October 1971 and which I will be revisiting next. Fearless is my favourite Family album still and in fact it is still my all-time favourite album by any band and as I write this I am really looking forward to reviewing it in detail.

I cannot remember exactly which Fearless songs were played that night but a guess would be Between Blue And Me, Children, Spanish Tide, Take Your Partners and as I sit here writing, an image of Roger Chapman swirling something in the air, making a weird bagpipe sound which is the song Blind and now I can hear him belting out the lyrics to what is a really heavy sounding song, so that song was definitely played I think.

The other things that sticks out in my memory is not sitting in our seats, we were standing, singing, the girls dancing as Roger Chapman thrashed wildly around the stage, mic stands being spun around and thrown but still his voice perfectly in harmony with the songs. Towards the end I think we moved to the front of the stage or were at least freaking out in the aisles, I guess this was rock Heaven for us, finally seeing our musical heroes live at last.

The memory you have just read would be repeated two (possibly three) more times, the third time being the Family Farewell tour and once again it was at the Newcastle City Hall, Friday 7th September 1973. A sad night but also a brilliant night which left all of our 'gang' wondering why Family were calling it a day, especially when they seemed to be at the height of their powers still, both live and in the studio but I will discuss this when I revisit their last album It's Only A Movie... life is only a movie isn't it?

The second time I saw Family, it was something of a curiosity, it was the 17th December 1972 and the government had decided to implement power cuts throughout the country which unfortunately interrupted Family's concert at the Newcastle City Hall. But this adverse situation has left a wonderful memory of the concert for me because even though for a short while there was no power in the hall and no lighting, Roger and the guys decided to play a short acoustic set with amplification while they waited for the internal power to return. I remember that candles were lit on the stage and Roger singing without a mic which was simply amazing I recall. I think that they performed for about twenty minutes if I remember rightly and the songs would have probably have been Processions, No Mule's Fool maybe, Holding The Compass and I definitely remember Children being one of the highlights. I also remember the crowd really appreciating Family for playing this acoustic set in the dim hall; I guess a lot of other bands would not have even attempted to do such a thing, many of them not having enough acoustic songs to sing possibly. A great memory then from a great live band, a band that a lot of other bands did not like to follow on stage at festivals, obviously because they were so brilliant live and that is a good indicator of how strong they were live.

Over the years I was to see Roger Chapman and Charlie Whitney live many times, both with Streetwalkers and The Shortlist but perhaps I will keep these memories until the end of this memoir.

The following picture is a photograph of me behind the guy at the front of Roger Chapman's concert at the Newcastle Opera House and the concert is available on dvd. That is me near the front with my arms in the air wearing my white FAMILY / CHAPPO t-shirt which I hand lettered myself in the FAMILY logo style, I only hope the picture prints here okay.

Life doesn't get much better than when you are at the front of a Chappo concert, his voice and stage presence and songs take over your soul completely and for the time of the concert all your worldly worries fade away. You really are taken back in time to the glory days of Family and your youth and then to the glistening possibilities of an optimistic future with Roger's brilliant solo songs which really deserve worldwide recognition. You will never find a better solo debut than Roger Chapman's CHAPPO album and then for me, his best solo album, the unbelievably brilliant KISS MY SOUL. I have to say here though, that of course all of Roger's albums are brilliant, the man just never ever lets you down. Why not check them all out, you will not be disappointed, I guarantee it. Cherry Red Records/Esoteric Recordings are currently releasing Roger's back catalogue and boy are they doing a fantastic job! The albums are simply a must-buy for any serious fan of excellent rock music.

Newcastle Opera House.

The John Peel Show, December 1971

One of my most precious possessions is my old battered Elizabethan tape recorder because on this tape still is a recording of the John Peel Show, broadcast on the 28th December 1971.

As I have stated earlier, I had seen Family live in November of this year so this Christmas treat was in the words of John Peel, "A real goody" and one which I simply had to try and record.

A much loved treasured possession that has somehow survived the test of time.

I cannot remember whether the tape was actually mine or not, it was just a family possession probably but somehow the recording has survived to this day, something my son James will eventually inherit and something that I hope he will treasure too considering how long it has been in the family... and yes, it still works!

This concert shows why Family remained a firm favourite with John Peel who championed them throughout their career and beyond with Streetwalkers. John Peel was a man who certainly recognised innovative music, Captain Beefheart being a firm favourite of his also.

The picture below is of the rare BBC Transcript disc of this John Peel show which is named Pop Spectacular which I bought years ago. I am pretty sure though that Family were never a 'pop' band, never really a 'singles' band, they were a serious 'album' band in the same way as let us say, Led Zeppelin was, as an example.

I probably bought this transcript disc from an advertisement in the music press and I seem to remember it was the Record Collector probably; it really felt at the time that I owned something valuable and rare and that was a great feeling, this brilliant concert is now available on the excellent Family at the BBC Boxset.

The banter between Peel, Roger and the studio audience is great and I do have the boxset cd to listen to now which is clear and of good quality and needless to say it ignites a great memory of mine as I do remember sitting quietly in the dining room, keeping everyone from passing through the room because I was taping the show, the microphone on the table, as close as I could get it to the radio and then frantically switching the tape reels over to catch the end of The Weaver's Answer.

The concert opens with the all-powerful Good News Bad News from Anyway then continues with Spanish Tide from their new album Fearless plus the hit single In My Own Time which should have been included on the LP and was included on the cd re-issue. The full concert track listing which John Peel comments is as follows:-

Good News Bad News - *"This week we have one of the best bands that we have in Great Britain and they are Family!"*

Spanish Tide -*"I was checking the BBC files earlier in the week and I found out that I have been doing programmes with Family longer than any other single group and if you heard that you will understand why."*

Part Of The Load - *"As an avid listener to the radio there seems to be too much chat on the radio so I will keep my announcements brief tonight, that was Spanish Tide and this is Part Of The Load."*

Drowned In Wine - *"Family are working well and the audience are working well and this is one you may remember from A Song For me..."*

Holding The Compass - *"This is from the LP Anyway, God bless you Dave..."*

Between Blue and Me - *"This is one of my all-time Family things... and Roger Chapman is going to play bass on this so listen carefully!"*

Children - *"Roger Chapman on bass and at no time did his hands leave his arms during that number."*

In My Own Time - *"Perhaps I should tell you who Family are, John Ken Wetton on bass guitar, guitar and vocals, John Poli Palmer on vibes, piano, congas, synthesiser, flute and cowbell which he plays with unusual sensitivity, John Charlie Whitney on Guitar, John Roger Chapman vocals, bass guitar and slide damage and John Rob Townsend on drums and stolen percussion."*

Take Your Partners - *"Take Your Partners, why not? Yes indeed, that's a real goody. Excellent stuff everybody!"*

The Weaver's Answer - *"This next one is a real treat..."*

Needless to say, this is one of my favourite Family recordings, Roger Chapman and the band in *"fine fettle indeed"* This really is one of the gems in my Family collection, something that always takes me back to better times whenever I listen to it.

Family Fearless

FEARLESS

October 1971

This album is dedicated
to all the people
who have pulled strokes
for or against us,
for they shall be called
fearless.

1

My mother Elizabeth bought Fearless for me with my own hard-earned money, after her early morning industrial nursing shift at the British Ropes factory at the Wheatsheaf in Sunderland. I was now in the Fifth Form at school and when I arrived home on the afternoon, the album was waiting there for me.

I think it was in the winter of that year that I started to work as a fitter's labourer at my mother's factory which was known locally as 'The Ropery' and this was a part-time holiday job that my mother managed to arrange for me, God bless her. This was a job that I would continue to have throughout my school and college days and one which would really help out financially, it was a great feeling being able buy a pint of beer with money you had worked hard to earn and as I write this now, I realise that this was probably the only job that I ever really liked.

I was still a Sunderland Boys footballer and my physical strength was to increase dramatically because of the hard labouring factory work. And it was hard work, pneumatic rock drilling by hand as I dug up factory floors for resurfacing and clearing the debris myself into skips, clearing out the 'rope walk' which was a long storage area for large industrial parts, painting the large silos on the factory roof which I have to say was a bit of a skive as a lot of sunbathing was enjoyed as we took turns to keep a look-out. I loved that labouring job, especially bombing around the factory on the stacker trucks and eventually I would only work with the best fitters, Tommy and Jackie Scullion. The fitter's would not work with many of the students and I was one of the few that they would trust so this gave me a sense of pride then and still does today. Actually, the factory bosses offered me an apprenticeship which I declined because I wanted to follow my art dream.

Another dream nearly came my way in the Sixth Form and that would come in the form of trials for Durham County School's football team. They played in a league that was followed exclusively by all the professional club's scouts. Unfortunately for me, I was injured before the trials, a pulled muscle in the back I seem to remember, probably from a badminton or basketball game or maybe even a volleyball game. This injury seriously affected my performance and another potential career path. My PE teacher Mr. Harrison did spray my back extensively with an ice spray which probably eased the pain but I simply could not perform to the best of my ability and I really should not have been playing at all. Mr. Harrison was adamant that I should have been included in that Durham County team, a route that would have possibly led to me becoming a professional footballer. Never mind, I still had my art and love of music, oh, and a few girls along the way too, girlfriends that I feel I never quite expressed myself properly to, probably due to immaturity and a deep inner shyness.

These were difficult times for me, my mother and father's marriage was on the verge of ending due to my father's heavy drinking. I realised a few years later that my father's alcoholism was probably due to his wartime experiences in Burma. He fought in the battle of Kohima which was recently voted by historians and experts as England's Greatest Battle because it stopped the advancing forces gaining entry into India. My father Charles was hit by a grenade and shot in the foot, God knows how many of the enemy he had to kill in that battle, and I am sure that he was suffering from Post Traumatic Stress all of his life after that, something that was not really discussed in his day but thankfully for today's soldier there is a greater awareness and understanding of it now.

So my family life was spiralling out of control now, I swapped girlfriend's a couple of times during this period as my mind was unsettled and worried. Looking back, I realise now that I could not focus properly, what I needed and craved was some sort of security because in the Sixth Form, my mother did leave my father and I went to live with

My father Charles.

My sister Dot and her son Andrew.

Charcoal drawing of my beloved Bengo, drawn many years later.

my sister Dot with my faithful dog Bengo. Another heartache for me was the death of Bengo during that year which took month's for me to get over, another factor which affected my mental stability at the time.

During my last year at school, I formed another relationship with a girl that I had known since junior school, I was now a young adult and this I felt to be 'real love' but once again Lady Luck decided that it was not to be and just before I was about to start my Foundation Art Course at

Sunderland Art College, the friendship finished, no arguments, no reasons… nothing. I began to spiral out of control again but there was one thing that was constant for me during those troubled teenage years and that was the music of Chapman and Whitney.

As I have stated earlier, Fearless is my favourite Family album and still my favourite album of all-time. Over the years many albums have threatened to nudge it from my number one spot though, the most recent being The Black Keys superb - Let's Rock.

But I am now trying to think of what other albums that were released that year that I would eventually add to my growing collection… The amazing Aqualung by Jethro Tull, Sticky Fingers by The Rolling stones, L.A. Woman by The Doors, Hunky Dory which is one of my favourite David Bowie Albums, Led Zeppelin IV, Split by The Groundhogs and Free Live, most of Free Live was recorded in Sunderland and I was there.

And of all the brilliant albums mentioned above, for me, Fearless shone the brightest, an album which is truly progressive though not 'Prog' as it is known today, an album produced by Family and their engineer George Chkiantz "who was always a big influence" according to Roger Chapman.

I am thinking back again now and I can see the sitting room of my house in Pennywell, my mother standing before me as she hands me the shopping bag that contained Fearless, she is smiling because she knows now how much the music of Family means to me. And after I had pulled the album out of the bag I must have just thought *Wow!* because here was another brilliant album cover. I would have seen the advertisements for the album in the music press but they would have most likely have been in black and white, not colour? Obviously, the first thing that hits you is the die cutting of the album. There are four extra 'flaps' to the front cover which open out like fans so that the album cover can actually stand up on its own. The background of the cover is white with a bold red outline going across the top then curving down the right hand side. On the first flap there are portrait images of the band in a royal blue colour going down from the top left corner to the bottom right. As the band's faces go along to the right, they merge with the other band members beneath until in the top right hand corner of the cover we have an abstract image of the band's faces combined in a distorted shape that could be described as an artistic logo for Family. This final distorted artwork of the combined band is a brilliant piece of conceptual art and was conceived by the talented designer John Kosh who would also design Family's next brilliant album cover for Bandstand. I seem to remember that both Fearless and Bandstand won design awards in the music press at the time with Bandstand appearing recently in the top 100 of album cover designs.

Above is the final combination of the band's faces, top right on the cover and above that we find Family, blue and small in a simple typeface, Futura I think, which gives the cover a very modern feel and the title Fearless is in the corner bottom right also blue, unconventional but that was Family, innovative and exciting, even with their album covers. I believe at the time, Family forked out about £10,000 for printing costs, once again they were thinking about their fans and not themselves.

The back of the album cover is in the same royal blue and top right we have a quote in an Old English style typeface - "This album is dedicated to all the people who have pulled strokes for or against us, for they shall be called fearless." Fearless was a term the band used at the time, "It's about those people who dared to stiff us or tried to pull a stroke" remembers Roger Chapman on the Mystic records cd, a cd that includes the hit single In My Own Time and the B-side Seasons.

Underneath the 'Fearless' quote at the bottom right of the album we have an intriguing small outline of a small creature, half rabbit half dog? Quietly walking along saying "Daft I call it" and I always wondered who came up with that and what exactly did it refer to and now I know from Roger that it was his opinion on the somewhat "pretentious" fearless quote.

2

Family were now in what I would call a 'New Progressive' mode, moving ever more away from that 'Summer Of Love' vibe but somehow still keeping it in some of the songs. But that was the way rock music was progressing and Family were leading the field in innovation and creativity. Roxy Music's game changing debut would be released in June of the following year and I like to think that maybe both Fearless and Bandstand was an inspiration to them, especially on their For Your Pleasure album where I personally see a great similarity to the song structures, dynamics, sound and song content. Maybe that is just me as both bands are important to me, I love them both and I do hear and see these similarities whether by coincidence or by chance or whatever, for that brief moment in time I think there was a definite similar feel to the brilliant compositions of Bryan Ferry and the brilliant compositions of Roger Chapman and Charlie Whitney.

3

Roger Chapman - Vocals, Guitars, Percussion, Harmonica and "coloured inner tube kind of thing."
Charlie Whitney - Guitars, Mandolin and Percussion.
Poli Palmer - Keyboards, Vibes, Flute and Percussion.
Rob Townsend - Drums, Paiste Cymbals and Percussion.
John Wetton - Guitars, Vocals, Contracts and Keyboards.

Brass - The Ladbroke Horns (who were actually The Average White Band.)

Produced by Family and George Chkiantz.

And now Family have another new bass player, now there are two double neck guitars. John Weider has left because he was 'tired of playing bass' I seem to remember reading somewhere, understandable I suppose because he was not just a bass musician.

John Wetton was a great addition to the band, coming on-board with a double neck bass guitar and what an image that was, two double neck guitar players which created a strong stage presence when they played two tracks from Fearless on the Old Grey Whistle Test tv programme, the two tracks being between Blue And Me and Spanish Tide. Something at the time did probably worry me though and that was the fact that for the first time now, there was no violin.

Family with no violin?

How is that going to work?

We shall soon see...

Between Blue And Me

Family always have great opening tracks on their albums and Between Blue And Me is no exception. The song is about a man and his friendship with a sailor. The man has not seen his friend for a year but he is reflecting in the waves of emotion caused by the sailor's wife cheating on him and the sadness of their small boy.

The song starts quietly with Chapman and bass guitar...

Road maps revive an old story

The song almost gliding along on rolling drums and floating guitar, the sound suggesting waves until two stronger wailing guitar lines break in and Chapman's intensity increases...

Waves of emotion, sea of joy
Times of sadness and one small boy

And the music seems to echo the sadness of the lyrics and Chapman's voice becomes suddenly angered...

His mother's a lady who forgets she's a wife
And she's making sure on a different score of life

Then the two guitars take lead, speaking and singing to each other then colliding together in the slow funk of the song that is driven by the drums. Chapman's powerful vocals are perfect for this emotional song until the lonely bass and the distant drums bring you down again, drums rolling again, guitars echoing and merging as one at the end.

Sat'd'y Barfly

Sat'd'y barfly is the song that first hints at the Americana vibe to come I think, a sound and feeling that Family would slip into for the next two albums and the following Chapman/Whitney song-writing album Streetwalkers. This is comfortable territory for Roger Chapman and the band get funky and drift back to a time of mohair suits, new white spats and smoky juke joints.

The song is basically about someone cruising down-town in a low slung cat on a Saturday night. When he spots a juke joint, he busts right in and there is Louise waiting for him and the party goes until 4am.

Funky open bar piano starts the song and then Chapman crashes in...

Well I was downtown cruising' in my low slung cat

A tuba is blasting somewhere in the background, over the western style piano, drums and percussion riding along then an outrageous whistle whoops when Chapman sees Louise and then that lonely tuba solo by Poli Palmer again, maracas accompanying it until we are back to that 4am groove...

We're drinking wine now, they ran out of gin
We're drunk as hell but we're feeling fine
If we leave now then we'll just have time

Then the tuba, whistle, soft guitar and is that the sound of a car or even one of those old biplanes? The band jamming, Chapman laughing...

Leave it out Louise, leave it out!

Larf And Sing

Poli Palmer really shines on this album and is included in four writing credits, two of them being his own compositions. For me, this where the sound of Family really becomes Chapman/Whitney/Palmer; a sound that would continue onto the equally brilliant next album Bandstand. I did read somewhere that the band had said to Poli that he should sing the lead vocals (?) on this track but listening to it again with earphones, I am quite sure that it is Roger Chapman, I do think though that Poli probably helps out with John Wetton for the chorus. Well, that is what I originally wrote but once again it is great to find out from Roger that it is Poli on all the vocals and all the instruments, how cool is that man.

This is a great 'feel good' song which includes a unique barbershop quartet style chorus line, something I feel that only Family could attempt and successfully achieve within the context of a rock song.

The lyrics to the song are quite deep, at odds possibly with the light vibe of the music and they come across as quite philosophical and acutely observational, *Life begins to write a book across my face*, which is an absolutely brilliant opening line.

The song deals with the problem of getting old, about life turning into a race and about feeling alone but we can still love and drink and larf...

There is a great rolling opening, Poli singing, almost whispering the lyrics in an up-tempo beat then that barbershop sounding quartet burst in...

That's why we all larf and sing
Whenever we all feel new

Then back to the beat, guitar gently floating vibe-like and then solo, almost singing as the song echoes away.

Spanish Tide

Spanish Tide is my favourite Family song, followed closely by How-Hi-The-Li and Good News Bad News. I would put these three songs up against any three songs by any band of that era or any era and I would play them to people who have never heard Family - the soft, haunting sound of How-Hi-The-Li, the creative dynamics of Spanish Tide and finally the awesome live power of Good News Bad News, three songs that are totally unique, totally original and totally Family.

Spanish Tide is quite a surreal song. I always think of it as someone looking out from their Spanish villa at the evening tide under a clear starry sky, possibly smoking a joint... which suddenly kicks in as the room folds around the man, the window, the mirror, a brightness holding the eye as the man finds himself standing beside the Spanish tide. And the stars are beguiling but he can only focus on one of them and as he comes down watching the tide turn, he realises that he is only part of life's circle and that the stars are only burning.

The dynamics of Family really shine on this song, slow start then it begins to rock in that unique Family style and beat, reaching its climax then coming down suddenly. John Wetton is great on this track and contributes to lead vocals which he handles really well.

Spanish style guitar opening, one lead, and one rhythm then joining together...

Slowly watch the tide turn
Far too late then we learn
There are only stars that are burning

Wetton joins Chapman, the music more intense with stop start rhythms, then harder drums crash in, vibes behind, louder, percussion rocking, Chapman harmonising perfectly and deliciously with Wetton.

Here it begins leading me on

Then a groovy beat as Wetton sings solo...

The brightest thing around the moon will darken as you cry

Then Chapman joining Wetton, power vocals, cymbals crashing then the vibes over them behind a spaced out guitar lead, vibes and guitar fighting until the music slows down...

Now it's for real, taking me down

The vibes twinkling like stars, the guitar mournful, piano punching out notes...

Circle years we could learn
There are only stars that are burning

And immediately you want to play the song again, hear it again, you want to be there beside that Spanish Tide.

With this song, Family prove that they still have that creative force within them and this is an album where once again the band are acting as a true solid unit, one that is experimenting with new ideas and new sounds using instruments found in the recording studio at the time. Yes, I guess for me, Fearless is probably their most experimental album considering it also has a new member with John Wetton. Bandstand would be just as creative but possibly here they would find their feet more as a band unit with a new member and it proves to be more solid and polished maybe, we shall see.

Save Some For Thee

After the dynamic high of Spanish Tide, Family crash in with a real brass rocker, horns prevalent from the start. This is a song about a man who is determined to take life slower, taking time to think about things more, trying to say what he is thinking and here we have more profound lyrics from Roger Chapman. And the slower the man takes it, the easier it all gets and he wants to save some of this wisdom for thee.

There is a thumping start, piano and thumping drums...

Took my life slower
So as not to fall over, no

Strong funky beat as Chapman sings, restraining his famous vibrato as the drums roll, piano punching...

Each day I try harder
To say what I'm thinking yeah

As the horns break in loud, almost announcing something then merging until Whitney's expressive guitar takes the lead, horns still behind...

But the slower I take it
The easier it gets me, yeah

Then only Chapman with horns behind...

As much as I carry
Is as much as I'm giving
You see

Then the song rolls away at the sound of a whistle, the horns dancing...

A great song that shows us once again what an amazing lyricist Roger Chapman is and it is another great song to sing along with and I always thought maybe it was solid single material.

Take Your Partners

And talking of experimentation and out and out funking rock, take your partners now for one truly hip freak out. One of my all-time favourites and another Poli Palmer co-write and his electronica really begins to shine here as he is given the freedom to let loose and really strut his stuff, I guess in a similar way as Eno does on the brilliant The Bogus Man from Roxy Music's For Your Pleasure but Take Your Partners is faster and more frantic.

Roger Chapman's lyrics are typically hard hitting here as he has a go at the critics...

The song rolls in, drums spitting, vibes asking questions in the background then a synthesiser blasts in ear-splitting then echoing as the beat of the drum increases, then the riff behind picks up, guitar speaking, then power chords as the music drives along in a great funky heavy beat.

Then Townsend's drums seem to announce Chapman's vocal intro...

God knows I'm hip
But I ain't yours or his
Everybody's arse is up for kicks

Crashing drums, diving piano, Chapman spitting out the lyrics; Family's famous rhythm style in-between. Then an echoey interlude, guitar lead backed by chopping chords, driving along and you are moving, dancing as the horns return, backing Whitney's great guitar solo, intensity building then stopping, drums crashing again then that diving piano...

Take your partners, what for?
Ain't you just kicked in the door
How come I don't believe you anymore

Then the vibes whistle, high pitched as the rock beat quickens as all the other instruments join in Family style and you are still rocking as the music fades, not wanting it to fade like so many other Family songs, you could move to this hip beat forever.

Children

This is an acoustic song, possibly a prelude to My Friend The Sun from Bandstand you might say as Family go into sing-along mode. The song is about a man observing his children and his family and learning from them as they play and sparkle before him, the innocence of youth is something that maybe we should all try to hold onto because all too soon it is gone from us. I think what we have here is Family trying to hold onto that hippy 'Summer of Love' vibe again and in that respect, the song really works.

Strong stuttering acoustic guitar begins to belt out an instant foot tapping rhythm...

Children can you laugh me
All your young life's meaning

Chapman softly sings showing the full extent of his vocal range as a chorus harmonises with him, guitar picking out singular notes. Then back to the beat...

Laa lala lala laaaah

Children is a short song but a poignant one which leads into...

Crinkly Grin

A short instrumental by Poli Plamer which has a great driving beat for bass and vibes and echoing guitar chords repeated, the vibes floating in the background in and out. There was a rumour that Roger Chapman had wrote lyrics for this instrumental and that the wonderful Elkie Brooks was also interested in extending it into a vocal song, both would have been great I am sure and a good testament once again to Palmer's versatility and creativity. A short interlude then before the power of Blind...

Blind

Blind for me is full on Family and Chapman, a song which I do find hard to define, to pin down, is it that 'gothic' thing again? Roger pushes himself to his limit here I feel as he sings about the horrors of people in pain, the sound of street violence and gun shots, cities on the verge of civil war. I always thought that there were bagpipes on this track but it turned out to be one of those "whirly coloured inner tubing things" said Roger Chapman that creates the whirring sound. The bagpipes were to appear on the next track though.

The song opens with that 'swirling inner tube' sound which is quite haunting then the guitar chords join in as the drums stomp along until...

Blind boy although you wish you could see
I've often thought if you could be me
Have eyes to see pictures of people in pain

Chapman not quite in frantic mode yet but it is building...

And it looks like I'll see them again, again

The sound soaring and Chapman's power rising, the beat picking up, that swirling sound growing until there is a break, horns, vibes and always the echo in the background and Chapman belting out the words, pushing himself to the limit. Then that almost Scottish sound dances into the slow come down of the song, I can hear bagpipes taking us down, echoing in the background as the song slows down and at the end there is only that empty, lonely sound that takes you straight into the metaphysical...

Burning Bridges

A hauntingly beautiful song which is yet another example of Roger Chapman's lyrical prowess and creativity, it is a song which is another slow burner as Roger grapples with the dangers of burning bridges on God's Holy Fire. This is another Poli Palmer influenced song which he is credited for and a fitting end to the most brilliant and best album I have ever heard. It is a modern gothic song for me which not many bands could emulate or get near to.

The song opens with a lonely guitar echoing again, waiting for Chapman...

Visions they're dancing like puppets on strings
Wait for the face in the choir to sing

And as the guitars follow Chapman's lead there is a dipping bass and the vibes merge behind...

Burning your bridges on God's Holy Fire
And all of the children you sire

As the bass become bolder, the haunting guitars spiral upwards, higher and higher and is that the bagpipes through a fuzz-box singing? The urgency of Rob Townsend's complicated beat picks up...

Of tall handsome strangers who pray down their nose
And they're nailed to the cross, I suppose

And Whitney's beautiful guitar picking out the floating notes as the song fades away. A magnificent song that makes you want to continue the Fearless journey you have just experienced.

In My Own Time

In My Own Time was released as a single a few months before Fearless and became Family's biggest hit, reaching number 4 in the charts. For me it is Family at their very best both creatively and commercially, I even remember now, older local hard lads, who did not really have much interest in progressive rock music I suspect, singing it out loud in the street as they walked past my house one day. And a great memory for me was my father whistling the tune as he put his tie on in preparation for a drinking session at the club, I remember that my friend Mick was in the house at the time and this just sent him into immediate hysterical laughter. My father was oblivious as to why we were laughing and continued to whistle In My Own Time as he left the house. Had I somehow brainwashed him with repeated playing of the song or is it simply a great catchy song that appeals to any generation? The latter I think.

And In My Own Time is a great song and deserved to be a number 1 hit but then again I am a bit biased. The B-side is a superb song called Seasons (That 'Summer of Love feel again maybe?) Roger Chapman in observational mode as he ponders the effects of the changing weather, a theme he would explore throughout his writing career.

With In My Own Time you are never going to get a more unusual innovative vocal opening to a song, and I do have it as my ring-tone on my phone which is always a head turner, Roger Chapman roaring out the rhythm like some demented choir singer and he does it twice for added effect then it is straight into a no nonsense powerful beat...

Lay down easy, stars in my eyes

(Which will be on my gravestone by the way...)

Try not telling too many lies

These lyrics are hard-hitting, memorable and straight to the point and the music compliments them perfectly with a beat you just cannot resist stomping along to, this is perfect hit material. There is a slight echo to Chapman's voice which is very effective and powerful...

Now some seek Jesus or flags they can wave

Won't touch nothing unless it's been saved

The guitars chopping away in the background blending perfectly...

You may think that I'm wasting my time

Think what you think

You know I don't mind

Chapman growls, the power intensity at a high level then just bass and drums...

I'll be with you in my own time

That takes us into a funky vibe break by Palmer, just right until Chapman's mad choir singer breaks back in, the beat grooving along, drums rolling and crashing, guitar perfect in the background...

In my own time, in my own time

I'll be with you ...repeated as it takes us out, Chapman rocking now like no other can until the strange wind-down sound of everything. Brilliant. Has to be one of the greatest ever rock singles and rock songs, Family at the top of their game and if you cannot get into and sing along to this song then I guess I have to feel sorry for you.

Review

Fearless reached number 14 in the album charts, down seven from Anyway but there had been a quite a gap in between studio albums which was filled by the Old Songs New Songs compilation and there had been another personnel change which had to effect the songs that had already been written in terms of getting them recorded. So the delay may have affected the sales somewhat, who knows, and Fearless is an experimental album of sorts for Family but experimental that works big time. Fearless should have been a number 1 album world-wide.

Suddenly the future held a multitude of daunting possibilities for the troubled teenager but I could always count on Family to lift my spirits. For me, Fearless is pure Family, even though the violin had gone, replaced by Palmer's electronica which is fresh sounding, contemporary and completely innovative. If you have never heard this album then put it on your 'must do' list immediately. Hip, dynamic, magical, mystical, metaphysical, intriguing, inventive, unique, original, powerful, soft, gentle, mystifying, experimental, 'new progressive' rock that was miles ahead of its contemporaries. Music for a new age and a new Family. Hell, I love this album, maybe you might give it a listen in its entirety, I guarantee that you will not be disappointed. Fearless is pure rock brilliance with a unique sound like no other, it is as simple as that.

Time for a cuppa I think...

October 1972

"There ain't a great many groups who have brought me pleasure every single time that I have seen them, five or six in fact… but there is one group I would travel continents to see perform and listen to… they are The Family." - John Peel, Family at the BBC.

1

1972 and the security that my young life had known was on the verge of spiralling away from me. My father was now a shadow of what he had been, an empty shell full of alcohol and nightmares. I sadly recall now, that a few years earlier, possibly 1969 as I seem to remember being about 14 years old, I had to stand between my father and my mother, they had been arguing, my father blind drunk and unstable had picked up one of the heavy metal candlesticks from the fire mantelpiece. I will always remember that look in his eyes as he looked at me, the awareness of what he had become and what he was about to do. He put the potential weapon down and then seemed to grapple within himself, obviously disgusted by his drunken actions. After that night, there never seemed to be any more violent arguments, there were arguments of course but they seemed sarcastic and mild by comparison to what had gone before. My father still continued to drink though as he became ever more detached from normal life. It was as if he had made some sort of decision to drink himself to death, that it would be preferable to the suffering, the inner turmoil and unwanted war memories that were surely tearing his soul and his mental stability apart. He spent more time in his beloved club than he did at home it seemed, it was like he had become an alcoholic zombie that only existed because of the club. But there is a happier ending to my father's story, one that I will probably mention later as this memoir unfolds but 1972 were days of darkness in Portrush Road and once again I was looking for things that would bring happiness in my life as I became a Sixth Former at school, the year of A-levels.

The A-levels I chose were Maths, Engineering Drawing and Art. Maths suddenly seemed to be a different subject, which was taught to me by a new teacher that I had always been a bit wary of. Engineering Drawing also seemed to be a new subject because my O-level was in Technical Drawing but Art was still one of the subjects that I loved even though we had to study History of Architecture which was interesting but hard to grasp at that age and the reason we did not study the great artists like Van Gogh and Picasso was because our art teacher Miss Dunn had studied architecture at college. So I went to Art College after the Sixth Form not knowing who Van Gogh or Picasso were; which must have seemed quite strange for my college tutor and peers at the time. Sunderland Art College was were I would meet my good friend Steve Nanson and I will always remember our first lesson together which was Life Drawing, Steve was standing next to me, we both had drawing easels, something that was obviously new to us both and when the model came into the studio and removed her dressing gown to reveal her naked body, we both looked at each other and smiled, I think I said something like, "This is good, think I might come back tomorrow." After that we became great friends and have remained so until this day.

I feel really proud to mention here that our brilliant life drawing tutor John Peace really liked my life drawings, so much so that he pinned them all on the wall in the life drawing studio and showed them to final year degree students. I am afraid that he seemed really upset that I decided to choose Graphic Design for my art degree course and had decided to stupidly leave Sunderland.

This really is another crossroads in my life where I made a massive mistake, if I had realised that I had a brilliant tutor wanting to mentor me in Fine Art I would have stayed at Sunderland Art College but I was an idiot but mainly driven by the thought that 'commercial art' would give me a job and that meant I could help my mother out financially. This was a big mistake as I ended up doing something I really did not want to do, Fine Art was I should have done, what I really loved but fate can be so cruel sometimes. Mr. Peace was not pleased with my stupid decision and I think he never talked to me again after I had told him what I was going to do Graphic Design.

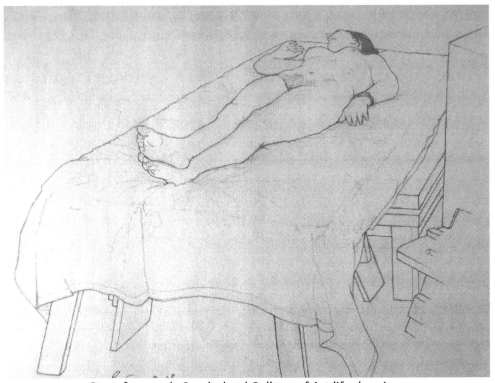

One of my early Sunderland College of Art life drawings.

I had my love of art then, my love of sport and as I have previously mentioned, my unfortunate Durham County football trials. I also had my love of music which was still extremely important to me and many other teenagers of my age. Two albums I remember buying that year was At Last by Free and the game changing self titled Roxy Music debut. I only bought the Roxy Music album because of an advertisement I had seen in the music press which I believe I have mentioned earlier and their music really was different at the time, experimental like Family and this appealed to me. The Roxy Music album would be a route I would follow, a pathway that would lead to The Velvet Underground and Lou Reed, David Bowie and the brilliant solo output of Brian Eno and that is another memoir.

Other albums released that year by bands I would appreciate more later were...

Exile On Main Street by The Rolling Stones which would become my favourite album of theirs.

Thick As A Brick by Jethro Tull, a concept album by Ian Anderson and a little dig at the critics I seem to recall.

Black Sabbath's Vol. 4 and School's Out by Alice Cooper, both favourites of Dickie Lincon, a good friend of mine and two albums we would listen to full blast, drinking ice cold Newcastle Brown Ale in his house opposite The Round Robin pub.

Other great albums were The Rise Of Ziggy Stardust by David Bowie, Transformer by Lou Reed and Harvest by Neil Young, all albums that I would add to my music collection later.

Captain Beefheart had become important to me that year and having bought his brilliant Strictly Personal first, I just had to buy both of his 1972 releases The Spotlight Kid and Clear Spot. Here was a blues rock voice as unique as Roger Chapman's and if you have never heard the Captain then these three albums are a must listen for you, blues based rock at its very best, you will not find better psychedelic blues anywhere. I seemed to be the only one at the time that liked Captain Beefheart and Roxy Music but I was not bothered by this and they are two bands that I still love today.

Family's album release that year then was the brilliant Bandstand, a name and concept conceived by their manager Tony Gourvish as the band seemed to be struggling to come up with anything. The album reached 15 in the UK charts and even dented the Top 200 in the USA starting at number 183 as that was the year they supported on the Elton John tour.

The song Burlesque was released earlier in August 1972 and was a big hit for Family reaching number 13 and staying for twelve weeks in the charts. They had recorded a version for Top Of The Pops and this version was aired while they were on tour with Elton John. Rob Townsend recalled that this version was not so good, Roger Chapman seemingly forgetting the words etc., and I think that this is the version I remember seeing and reading about. The Top Of The Pops producers wanted Family to mime the song but Family would have none of it, apparently they came to agree that Family would record the song live for the show during the day then on the night, Roger would sing live over the recording. Of course after a few beers later while they waited, the band came on and Roger messed around, probably showing a bit of contempt for the whole 'pop' business. It's a great memory for me and a real laugh and I think the band had a lot of fun that day at the Top Of The Pops expense. Needless to say, I have never seen that version again and it is suspected that Top Of The Pops and the BBC have deleted it.

When the song became a hit and after they had returned from the States, the band recorded a more 'respectful' version which is still available to see today. However, Burlesque might not have been a hit as the band did not think of it as a single at first. The Who were recording in the Olympic studios in Barnes at the same time and Pete Townsend came into the Family mixing room and heard Burlesque and straight away said that it should be a single, Keith Moon also came in and heard the song and said simply, "That's a winner!" and so Family released Burlesque as a single and the song is now one of Family's most well known and loved songs, always played live and always a crowd favourite.

Another 'winner' for Family that year was the Bandstand album cover which was once again designed by the brilliant designer John Kosh aided by photographer Peter Howe.

The front cover is the front of an old bakelite fifties television set on which it displays a blue tinged photograph of the band in the studio on its screen. It looks late at night and Roger Chapman, Rob Townsend and John Wetton look a little fed up and tired as they sit waiting for Charlie Whitney and Poli Palmer who still seem to be working away. You half expect Roger Chapman to stand up at any moment and declare, "Don't know about you guys but I'm off down the pub!" I think that the image is great and atmospheric and does hint at what working in the studio can really be like.

Below the tv screen image, in between the television controls is the new Family logo, an art deco style typeface in yellow that is perfect for the era implied and a cool logo style too I have to add.

Bandstand is a double sleeve fold out album and when you open it, you realise that the title Bandstand is printed on transparent plastic and the photograph of the band is on the tube inside, you are now looking at the inside of the television set which is very clever and very innovative design. The back of the album is what you would expect, the back of the television complete with wires, tuning and contrast controls. No wonder then that this album cover won music press awards for design; it is absolutely brilliant and absolutely original.

But what would the music be like? John Wetton was still a member of Family and they had become tighter as a unit, both on the road live and in the studio. Would the album be able to top Fearless? For me it comes very, very close and I guess Fearless pips it only because of its fresh experimental quality.

As I have pointed out earlier I do think of Family now in terms of pairs of albums which depend on the band personnel, the fourth pairing being

It's Only A Movie and Streetwalkers, Streetwalkers being kind of like Family's 'lost album' because most of the songs would have definitely have been on it I think. So I have divided Family into four segments from the start, Family Mark 1, 2, 3 and 4, each segment vital to the continuing creativity and each segment favoured differently by their legion of fans. I guess for me I would have to go for Mark 3 and 1 but with Family's albums it always changes depending what sort of listening mood I am in.

The bandstand is ready then, the band is about to start playing and I am now off to Bandstandland…

2

Roger Chapman - Vocals, Percussion, Harmonica.
Charlie Whitney - Guitars.
Poli Palmer - Keyboards, Vibes, Flute and Percussion.
Rob Townsend - Drums and Percussion.
John Wetton - Guitars, Vocals and Keyboards.

Vocal Assistance - Linda Lewis.

London String Arrangements - Del Newman.

Produced by Family and George Chkiantz.

Burlesque

Burlesque is basically a song about hitting the town for a good time and ending up in the Leicester Burlesque club, rolling and tumbling along with Rita and Greta and like how Lou Reed would imply in his songs, you always get the feeling that these are real people who Roger Chapman knew. Burlesque is a heavy, hard hitting song that makes you get up on your feet and dance and sing along and this was what Family were surprisingly good at you might say, they produced songs that made you want to sing along with them. And that was their genius, a lot of their songs were not songs that you could immediately hum along to and I think John Peel mentioned something along these lines about their compositions, they were not songs that were easy to write, lightweight pop song, no, they were progressive rock songs that were serious album songs not written to be fickle pop hits. The brilliant J.J. Cale would one day admit that just about all the songs he wrote were meant to be singles but Chapman and Whitney did not operate like that and they did suffer from a poor choice of single material now and then as I have mentioned earlier. Let's sing along to Burlesque then...

Yeah

Solid drums and jagged Whitney trademark guitars open the song...

Rolling and tumbling ain't done me no harm

Gonna boogie my night owl away

And the heavy funky riff grabs you straight away, Chapman's vocals powerful; the guitar riff echoing... and the guitar gets heavier, fuzzier as Chapman rolls and tumbles along to the beat, the bass guitar rasping behind him...

Drinking, stinking

Just been too bad on my arm

Guitar and Chapman interplaying, while the song grooves along. Rita and Greta finally leave but Chapman's not alone and he has *been kinda sneaky* to get her alone...

Result.

This is yet another great opening track, another original song that showcases the uniqueness and individuality of the Family beat, a well deserved hit.

Bolero Babe

Gently fading in after the power of Burlesque is another favourite of mine, the spaced out Bolero Babe which could have easily appeared on Fearless with its strong haunting synths, flute and strange sounds like the tapes running backwards, Family back in studio experimental mode. The song is one of those magical drifting songs that make you want to float away with it as the intensity builds slowly and Roger Chapman is in familiar lyrical territory as he dreamily thinks about the past, suggesting space, light years shining, near and far...

Light sensitive drums, whirling synths slowly fade in...

Just million of miles
To gaze at life's smiles that's surrounding us

Chapman in light tranquil mode then punctuating, emphasising his words...

I can see it shine
Light years from here

As the strings break in with a pulsating bass bopping in the background, drums still rolling...

We've got thousands of ways
Of counting the days, as they pass us by
They're here then they're gone
And they won't linger on, will they babe?

Chapman harmonises beautifully and the music responds as the climax builds...

How near
Yet how far

Strings stomping along, backing vocals crying *Far... Far...* as the song fades and curls into the gentle sounds of...

Coronation

Here we find the band in nostalgic, melodic mode that immediately transports you back to another era, another time, that house were Family lived and the characters there, Dr. Sam and Jenny. Roger Chapman paints a picture, contemplation, a memory, like a novelist writing descriptive gems. You are bewitched by this enchanting song and its enticing spell that takes you back in time with it.

A beautiful piano opening complimented with vibes and a slow solid beat...

Evening and I'm sitting here
Though I've got some things to do

Chapman's voice floats along as the tempo increases then the chorus, strong and bold with a foot stamping beat...

Pictures crooked on the wall

Clothes they lay where they fall

Into the musical interlude with vibes, synths, xylophone, floating as the strings break in with Whitney's guitar into that stomping beat that breaks down again...

Oooh, I've got to move again

Seems like I've been here too long

Back into the chorus, that suddenly whirls away Family style. A beautifully emotive song that really displays exactly how great Family were.

Dark Eyes

This is a short song that always cries out to me to be a longer track; written by Whitney/Palmer, lyrics by Roger Chapman, chords by Poli Palmer. A beautifully romantic song, intimate and poetic about two lovers in the shadow of the evening, a suggested sadness but we will never know why.

A lonely piano opens, then faster acoustic guitar...

Dark eyes that question

The sadness that is now

Chapman beautifully gentle and in complete harmony with the emotions of the song. The beat is faster than you think as the flute and piano float, guitar in the background, taking you along as it fades away way much too soon, almost like a fleeting glimpse of something that you have been fortunate to observe and experience.

Broken Nose

And after the romantic gentle sounds of Dark Eyes, your mood is instantly changed by the raw powerhouse that is Broken Nose, Family checking out of side one on an incredible rocking high.

The song is about wanting something that you cannot have and when you finally get it, you wish that you had not. The femme fatale with **diamonds on her fingers and rhythm in her ass,** the woman that initially ignores you, teases you because you are not worthy, and we have all known women like that surely? And then one day the woman becomes suddenly vicious for no apparent reason, suddenly violent and that is when you stop loving her.

I now remember a similar vicious moment when I was at college, I had been arguing with my 'girlfriend' then she suddenly attacked me and like an idiot I let her hit me, repeatedly hard on the head and face, stupidly thinking because I was young and strong that I could easily take it. Then as the blows increased, I realised that I was sort of losing consciousness so I had to make her stop. I suffered an immediate amnesia from the attack and for a short while I could not remember my name, which was very scary let me tell you. From that day onward I decided that no woman or man for that matter; would ever hit me again, you have to protect yourself, no matter who it is. Maybe she broke my nose too?

Chiming guitars build at the start of the song then Chapman crashes in...

Seen her everyday now and boy has she got class
She's got diamonds on her fingers and rhythm in her ass
Drums rocking as Linda Lewis sings in the background...
I like your
Dig your
Chapman's vocals are raw, the beat frantic...
The day that I stopped loving you
Was the day you broke my nose
Then a swirling bass interrupted by a swirling synth solo that is manic Roxy Music Eno style or maybe that should be Family Poli Palmer style. Then back to the driving rock beat, bass pulsating ominously until...
She said ahdo and grabbed my cue
And shoved it dddd down my throat
The band really rocks out, synth blaring, Linda Lewis howling beautifully, guitar dancing as the synth holds it all together.

Before cd's you had two sides of vinyl so it made sense to finish side one with a song that makes you want more and boy does this song do that in spades. And when you immediately flip the record over, you are once again greeted by a change in mood and tempo, proof again of just how breathtakingly creative Family are.

My Friend The Sun

Here we have an immediate change of pace with light, acoustic and brilliant guitar by Charlie Whitney. My Friend The Sun was a single released in December 1972 but failed to chart significantly which is a total and utter mystery to me and every other true Family fan. It is another of those great Family sing-along songs, if not their greatest and a good choice for a single but the pop charts are fickle and somehow for whatever reason, it was overlooked. A real damned shame because this song had the potential (and still does) to be a massive hit, not just in the UK but world-wide and that is no exaggeration. The song today is widely covered by amateur and professional artists alike and two I can think of immediately are the talented Linda Lewis and Jimmy Nail.

This is the song on this album, maybe along with Bolero Babe, where Family are once again paying homage to that hippy groove, another Roger Chapman lyric about the changing weather and how it is always possible to change your circumstances...

It's never too late

Beautiful floating acoustic guitar chords open the song...

Well I know that you're lonely come in from the cold
Your shoes they need mending your clothes they look old

Chapman sings ever so gently but it is understated restrained power as always for songs like this...

Although there's been rain and it's coming again
Change has to be here obviously

Then synth vibes accompany Chapman and Whitney's guitar...

Though my friend the sun looks well on the run
He's there in the distance, if you care to see

A wonderful synth breaks in, coasting along with the guitar, then the harmonies, dipping and diving making you want to sing along...

If season were reason then there'd be no doubt
A sequel of changes worth putting you out

And then John Wetton joins in the background vocals until the song suddenly winds down...

The sun is here at last, shining brightly in your soul; that is how the song makes you feel.

Glove

And the tempo remains laid back on the next track, a slow building one that once again displays the prowess and range of Roger Chapman's vocals and the quality of the band. Glove is another song that seems to transport you back to another time when men were gentlemen and ladies wore gloves and took innocent walks in summer breezes, and here we have one lucky man who is given the chance to walk along with one of those enticing ladies.

A solitary bass line slowly picks out the opening line then Chapman harmonises with it...

Oh I picked up a lady's glove

I gave it back to her and she put it on

Then Rob Townsend's drums rattle in as the temp increases, piano in the background...

Then the question seemed to turn out wrong
Because I quietly swore and bit my clumsy tongue

The music gets louder as the strings back Chapman's harmonies and the most beautiful guitar by Whitney, quiet then loud as we go back to the main theme and the intensity increases, the strings and backing music brilliant, Whitney's guitar is also brilliant as he displays his superb solo ability here as Chapman sings in the background...

She said 'walking' then taking care
She brushed her cheek
Where the summer breeze
Had caught her hair

Soft and gentle then Chapman lets loose...

I'd be so pleased of you'd
Accompany me to walk awhile

Wonderful, brilliant, Family band dynamics at their very best.

Ready To Go

Then the mood and the tempo changes again as Roger Chapman decides to have a go at those negative critical people we all come across in life. This is another of my favourites and once again I find myself writing about a great rocking song that you can sing along with.

Straight away the band are into a funky beat announced by Townsend's brilliant rapping, rolling drums and Whitney's signature guitar sound...

I'm ready and able
To shove all your labels below

And Chapman is in mischievous mood as he sings...

Just choose a word careful
Cos I've got a handful of crap I can throw

Then the chorus that I really love and you want to sing with Chapman instantly, vibes in the background...

I've been down the line
And I've served me some time

Choppy stop start then back to the main theme, synths, guitars echoing the vocals, stop start then the guitar break, the drums really rocking. What a sound Whitney has on his lead breaks, he is probably the most underrated rock guitarist of all time, but not by me. Then we are back singing...

I'm hungry and howling
Can't quit this scowling today
I've seen down the cracks
Of all of you Jacks -
And I'm ready to go

And you think the song is finished but it twists back into that marvellous Whitney lead groove that sadly eventually has to fade.

Top Of The Hill

Top Of The Hill is another song that displays the genius of Family's dynamics. A slow builder that effortlessly takes you along with as it gathers momentum and once again there is a chorus that makes you want to join in with it. Roger Chapman is in deep thought mode again as he ponders the absurd in life and the memories we all have, **but if you're looking for time, you'll be looking until, there ain't no crying at the top of the hill...** and we all know that it is Boot Hill he referring to, the end of the line for us.

This is a song that plays with your emotions, inviting you to reflect on what has been good in your life and what has been sad, **but they're never so bad if you grin.** Remain optimistic but always remember the final outcome

A quiet bass line opening with floating vibes that build slowly, the drums punctuating the moment then the music hits a rhythm as the intensity builds and the guitars burst in with Chapman...

You can do most things when how you want

The chords crashing as Chapman sings about... **clowns in the ring and all the ladies you've ever seen** as the music dips again, the guitar urgent then the orchestral strings and a distant bass groove along in the background...

There ain't no crying
At the top of the hill

A lonely xylophone accompanies Chapman until the grand sound of the twenty piece orchestra takes over until the sudden stop.

Review

The band are definitely tighter on this album, the songs maybe less experimental than Fearless but the quality of song-writing is exactly the same leaving most of their contemporaries at the time behind in the dust. Bandstand is another highly creative album full of emotions of every kind. The songs and lyrics are incredible, quiet ballads, out and out rockers, funky rhythms, imagery and music that is capable of transporting you to other times, other places, other memories. This is what Family can do; they can take away the worry and strife of your normal life, if only for a short while until you play the record again.

Like the first incarnation of Family, if this band had stayed together then who knows what heights they would have achieved? But this is Family; things were destined to be never straight forward for them. John Wetton was to leave and join King Crimson then to be tempted by those 'bright new shiny things' that were Roxy Music, possibly a good personal career move for him (although I do not know how you can top being in Family) but not for Family.

1973 would prove to be a fateful year for Family.

And a year of change for me.

But life is only a movie... isn't it?

My Family shelf for my cd's and dvd's etc.

September 1973

"Well we certainly didn't record it with a feeling that it was going to be the last album, or that we were going to split up. I was pleased to have Tony and Jim onboard, and like before the new members brought a new musical direction." - Roger Chapman.

1

1973 was a bitter sweet year for me, sweet because later in the year I would fall in love, what I felt was real love at the time. A bitter year because Family decided to disband and yet for me, their final album is a triumph, it does not sound like an album where the band are just going through the motions because at the time of the recording, the decision to call it a day had not been made. In fact, Family had started their own record label called Raft and had released the album through it. I guess the warning sign may have come from the single selected from the album; Boom Bang/Stop This Car released in April of that year which did not make the charts. Boom Bang was probably a poor choice in retrospect with radio unfriendly lyrics and a hard to describe rhythm. I think Boom Bang is an absolutely great sort of slow burning blues driven song that is totally unique and original but releasing it as a single at the time of the rise of glam rock was probably not a good move. In September 1973, Family released Sweet Desire as a single and here we have a much better choice but I guess it may have been too long between hit singles for the song to achieve the success it deserved. The B-side, Drink To You is a great Jim Cregan penned rocker which features Linda Lewis in fine form accompanying Family once again.

John Wetton had left to join King Crimson and this was followed by the departure of Poli Palmer which was a shock for many long time Family followers. There had some talk about Poli delving deeper into electronica with his synths and vibes and the band consensus was that it would effect the band live, setting up programmes etc. As I have said earlier, with Fearless and Bandstand I feel that they were heading into Roxy Music For Your Pleasure territory before Roxy Music would even get there and I still believe today that that they should have continued in that art-rock vein, although I am not sure what Poli Palmer would have looked like in make-up, silver sequins and feathers or Roger Chapman for that matter ha-ha, Family fitted out in glam rock fashion? I don't think so.

But as we know now with Family, new band members always meant changes in music and direction for Family and It's Only A Movie was no exception. Tony Ashton replaced Poli Palmer and Jim Cregan replaced John Wetton and Roger Chapman and Charlie Whitney were becoming more intrigued and interested with the Americana vibe they were getting into. Jim Cregan is a highly accomplished talented guitarist and would eventually work with Rod Stewart and Tony Ashton was a rocking piano player and both fitted comfortably into the 'good times' direction they were heading in, a sort of fun-time feel especially live, I guess similar to what the Faces were advocating at the time. Family had quite simply decided to have fun and sod the consequences and were still an amazing force live.

I was at their Farewell Tour concert in Newcastle on the 7th September, my final time of seeing Family but by no means my last time of seeing Roger Chapman and Charlie Whitney live as I will recall in the next chapter. For a band that had decided to call it a day, they were brilliant and they had a great final album so the obvious question for me and my friends at the time was why? I guess it all came down to not cracking the USA market maybe, like their lesser contemporaries, a tour there in 1973 fell through because Jim Cregan and Tony Ashton had commitments elsewhere. Lack of chart success with no recent hit singles and It's Only A Movie only reaching number 30 in the album charts did not help too, these must have been the final nails in the coffin so to speak but also I think now, maybe Roger and Charlie needed a new challenge, one that would inspire their creative juices again?

I was now in the Sixth Form at school and we had our own large common room which was next to the music department so we were allowed to play records during our free periods and at lunch times. Most of my old school friends had left to enter the real world of work and I was still factory labouring during the holidays but new friendships were formed with people who had come from other schools because their school did not teach at A-level. I have to say that that I do not recall many of them who knew of or actually liked Family in the Sixth Form but I used to play It's Only A Movie a lot in the common room and it became really popular (as did the following Streetwalkers album) and 'Movie' gained new fans for the band... so there was the irony, perhaps they were heading in the right direction and perhaps their decision to disband had been made too soon?

I remember buying other albums that year and one of those was Free's final album which was suitably called Heartbreaker. I love Free and Paul Kossoff remains my favourite LEAD guitarist, closely followed by the brilliant Jimi Hendrix, Phil Manzanera and obviously the unique style of Whitney, and Charlie, you are the Riff King for me and your lead playing is simply sublime and so original and I guess as the 'complete guitarist' there are not much better. The decision for Free to quit, possibly because of Paul Kossoff's continual battle with the drugs which would sadly lead to his untimely death was another bitter moment for me and obviously thousands of others.

The other album I bought that year was the brilliant For Your Pleasure by Roxy Music which was released on 23rd March 1973. Another album bought for me with my money by my mother on her way home from work I seem to remember and I do recall holding it in the house for the first time and having the same level of excitement within me as when I had first looked at Fearless only two years earlier. Strange isn't it, when you think back, you do not realise how fast time is actually passing you by when you are young.

Like Family, Roxy Music always had great album covers, a cover girl being a continuing theme with Roxy Music and the For Your Pleasure cover is exceptional. A dark night time picture with a glamorous model holding a panther on a lead and behind them in the distance is a futuristic, glowing cityscape. The picture extends across to the back of the album where chauffeur Bryan Ferry waits beside a black limousine. And as I have already stated, I find the music of this album similar in style, structure and dynamics to the songs of Fearless and Bandstand and For Your Pleasure remains one of my top albums of all time.

Other albums of that year I would come to buy later were Dark Side Of The Moon by Pink Floyd, Goodbye Yellow Brick Road by Elton John, Selling England By The Pound by Genesis, Berlin by Lou Reed, Passion Play by Jethro Tull and I have to say that at the time I was beginning to think that maybe Jethro Tull were getting a bit too conceptual for me but as I write this I really feel like revisiting this album. Other albums were Houses Of The Holy by Led Zeppelin and I have to say that for me they were beginning to possibly lose it here maybe (Sorry Zepp fans) but they did regain 'it' in spades with the release of 1975's brilliant double sided Physical Graffiti, which would become a great favourite of mine. An album that my college friend Dave Williams would play regularly in his car along with The Rolling Stones Get Your Ya Ya's Out, Let It Bleed and Exile On Main Street, The Beach Boys and Buddy Holly because we were beginning to live the Americana dream, in the way we dressed, thought and acted, Dave was like a mixture of James Dean and Kowalski from the cult road movie Vanishing Point, cowboy boots and brown leather jacket and red check shirt which he never seemed to take off, we really were two young cool dudes in those days.

Me (first left) and Dave and college friend, hard at work playing table football.

Another great favourite album of mine which I would buy during my first years as a college student was the exceptional Sabbath Bloody Sabbath by Black Sabbath. 1976 and I was a student in London now, having transferred from a college I liked but a first year tutor who was unbelievably negative towards me and my artistic ability, boy was he dull and uninspiring with no idea of contemporary art at the time or anything creative.

But suddenly now though, I now found myself in a despondent, depressive one room bedsit that had a small un-open-able window that looked out onto a tiny claustrophobic overgrown garden and an endlessly drab white skyline. I argued too much with my 'girlfriend', I ate too little, I drank too much and I fought too much. I do not know whether it was my black leather motorbike jacket and subsequent fifties rock and roll imagery, Brylcreem and all, that was somehow getting me into a constant cycle of violent confrontations but all I know is that I never lost a fight during those dark dangerous days. I even beat a locally known so-called amateur boxer who was much taller than me and someone who consequently kept out of my way whenever he saw me in the street afterwards ha-ha. I guess all my football and all the hard labouring work had paid off for me. (For more drunken violence please see my Roxy Music Eno memoir which is the start of my art college days.)

I was becoming no Bruce Lee though and these years of not eating properly and drinking too much did slowly take their toll on me in my final college year. I did pass my degree though but only just, as I managed to get my act together for a few weeks in order to put up some sort of a degree show of work.

So I guess I realise now that in that disheartening bedsit room I was beginning to experience the first bitter taste of depression and I guess I regularly yearned for home and the security of my labouring job. Why I never quit my degree course and went back to Sunderland Art College to study Fine Art, something that I really loved, is beyond me. I have mentioned early that I probably would have become a successful artist by being taken under the tutorial wing of renowned local artist and art teacher John Peace. So once again things might have been so much better for me but maybe that is another reality because for years now I have said that I think I am stuck in The Wrong Reality, a saying that has recently manifested itself as one of my published novels.

Anyway, one day I found myself browsing through a small second-hand record shop near to where I lived at the time and I came across the Sabbath Bloody Sabbath album and immediately I was hit by memories of my friend's house opposite The Round Robin pub in Sunderland. Black Sabbath was my friend Dickie Lincoln's favourite band and we had listened a lot to their music during many a drunken night in his house. I have to say though, that I was not a big Sabbath fan at the time, their music being 'guitar heavy' compared to Family and their eclectic instruments. I guess I also thought that Ozzy Osbourne's lyrics were a bit too depressing and doom laden at the time although I did really get to like Sabbath's Volume 4 which sounded more optimistic and up-beat to me.

I did have a small portable record player when I was art college which makes me wonder now about what happened to it, it must have ended up in my mother's house but for some reason it did not survive like the old tape recorder.

I was not sure what Sabbath Bloody Sabbath was going to be like when I first played it but thinking back now I was determined to like it because somehow I instinctively knew that it would help my state of mind. I need not have worried though, Sabbath Bloody Sabbath is a classic album and still what I call a 'top ten' album for me, I loved it and still do and it did help me get through the loneliness of that depressing bedsit by making me recall happier times, so thank you Ozzy et al.

2

But let us return to 1973 again and the enigmatic It's Only A Movie. Straight off I have to say that listening to it today, it still sounds as fresh and maybe even better than it did in 1973 but if you were to ask most long-time Family fans, many would probably say that it is their least favourite album by Family maybe and I can only conclude that this is because the consistent creative standard of Family is so high possibly and I think now that I am sure that that my fellow Sixth Formers would disagree that it is their least favourable because this is were they came on-board as regards the songs of Chapman and Whitney.

Again the album cover design is striking, designed once again by the ever brilliant John Kosh and again the string and brass arrangements are by Del Newman and the main engineer is the loyal George Chkiantz. So the same successful background team was in place which you have to say, is at odds with the relatively low level of success it achieved.

On the front cover we have an old western movie star and I am certain that it is Tom Mix in black and silver celluloid, big western ten gallon hat, large neckerchief and two guns pointing straight at you. You can almost imagine him saying, "You don't like Family? Then stick 'em up you varmint!" then bang bang!

The title is top right with FAMILY in bold capitals, light blue with a thin pink border and once again not the FAMILY logo that would become their trademark. Underneath we have the album title and the colour is reversed, the colours work somehow against the silverish background and now I cannot imagine any other colours being used.

The back cover is a great montage of the band members in action, Charlie reaching a high point during a solo with his double neck guitar and Roger funking out with a Fats Domino t-shirt. Jim Cregan looks studious and reflective and Rob Townsend looks ever optimistic on drums, while Tony Ashton looks almost vampiric on piano.

Inside the album there was a paper 'banger' I do not know what happened to mine, probably lost or stolen at some drunken party. The back of the inside record sleeve displays all of the song lyrics, a trait that Family had started with A Song For Me and on the other side in keeping with the western theme, is an old drawing and advertisement for a Weston pistol - New Single Action Frontier and Peacemaker. Every one warranted. (Regular price $16.00.) See our price.

Family used to come on stage to the theme music of the western movie, The Big Country and this time they were going out six-guns blazing, that is exactly how I remember it, going out in style with a great album and great live performances. Come on, what else would you expect from the brilliant and wondrous band known as Family?

3

Roger Chapman - Vocals, Percussion, Harmonica.
Charlie Whitney - Guitars.
Rob Townsend - Drums and Percussion.
Jim Cregan - Guitars
Tony Ashton - Piano and Vocals.

String and Brass arrangements by Del Newman.

Produced by Family.
Engineers, George Chkiantz, John Middleton and Rod.

It's Only A Movie

This song does exactly what it says on the tin, it is about the making of an old western movie featuring Tom Mix maybe from the front cover and basically it is loosely about the conflict between the director and the leading actor who just wants to ride away into the sunset with Kitty the cowgirl on his big charger, "Yee haw!"

A swirling piano then a wailing guitar riff start with a sound like a horse galloping, the reel rolling then back to the plonky bar-room piano…

Cards on the table at midnight (Chapman laughs)
Watch for the hand with the blade

Ashton opens but Chapman responds in a class vocal duet while the beat rocks along with the same guitar riff then the funky piano…

Two evils can never make one right
The Chapman chorus sings…
But be sure one evil has already been done
Responds Ashton the storyteller.
This is a great stomping rocker with a chorus that you just have to sing along with again…

It's only a movie, it's only a show
Then funky deep horns break in that glide along with the rhythm into a solo break then Whitney's guitar again that takes you back to the story break…

That crooks gotta bleed to make them want more

And the song rocks out with the sound of galloping horses, gunshots, cowboys shouting and howling, horses whinnying and wailing into the distance...

Another great album opener from Family who are shooting from the hip here, right from the start.

Leroy

Chapman and Whitney continue their journey into Americana with a song set in the fifties, about Leroy and his quest for the rich Campus Queen so that he can finally get the car of his dreams. And he does, he gets the girl and the car, "Yee haw!"

There is an acoustic opening to the song with a wailing harmonica by Roger Chapman, who I have to say is one brilliant harp player; then he begins to sing gently in that American accent he seemed to be naturally acquiring and developing for these songs.

The chorus describes the car that Leroy craves...

He craved a flat top winner, with a 2 spot dimmer

While accompanied by lush strings and rich vocal harmonies, the string's swirling in the background and the drums hopping around in a funky style. Chapman's enchanting harmonica is prominent, Whitney on slide style guitar responds; then the chorus takes us out with those haunting strings again.

Buffet Tea For Two

My guess that the favourite track on the album for most people, especially the long time fans; would be this song and what a great epic this is with those rich string arrangements again. Family use of strings on their songs is far superior to any other band I can think of and for me there cannot be a better vocal harmoniser than Roger Chapman.

Is this Family's final lingering hippy style song? Possibly and that forever cool vibe was fading fast throughout rockdom at this time. This is another song that evokes nostalgia for me; you really are there on that train experiencing the emotions implied. The song is indeed an emotional ride, a song about someone getting onto a train to make a new start in a new city but at the expense of leaving his loved one behind.

This is definitely a song that harks back to the old Family with that wonderful building dynamic that they were so good at, creative song-writing at its very best.

Charlie Whitney's humming dancing guitar opens then drums and a brass section blasts in over it, Chapman's voice is restrained as the story starts...

Buffet tea for two, a farewell kiss for you

Then the rhythm picks up, floats along until the horns clash in again and Chapman picks up the tempo...

To a new start, a new city
Leaving you my pretty

And Whitney's guitar sounds sad and lonely, just right for the song as ever. There is a brilliant piano break in the middle while the music and tension builds slowly behind, choppy, dancing, faint vocals, the strings urgent leading into another superb guitar break by Whitney that leads into the final passage, the man arriving at his destination...

Yes Pancras here I come
I raced them all and won

As the music crashes back, stop start, taking us out of the song into the opening chorus of the next song...

Boom Bang

This is a song that I always find hard to describe as I have mentioned earlier, a sort of slow funk with a definite blues feel. It has the indefinable Family quality that sort of gets under your skin, a sort of erotic film noir about a man who sounds sexually frustrated, all hay-wired with those tempting tv nudes running constantly through his head...

Whoa I'm sick and tired, all hay-wired
Fever that's for sure
Moon, lune girl erection for a cure

Wails Chapman as he spits out the words, Whitney's guitar backing him, the drums stamping at intervals. Then back to the frustrations of the shady guy as the vibes and the backing vocals cry out...

Boom bang, shotgun man
I said I feel as if I'm dead

And the music twists to one of those sudden Family endings.

A totally unique song that that definitely grows on you and a pointer towards the Streetwalkers direction maybe.

Boots 'n' Roots

Side two of the record opens with another western style song that could have easily have graced the floorboards of the Grand Ole Opry. A simple but descriptive song about a lone man just riding along, maybe it is that guy with his ol' mule again, they were nobody's fools. My original vinyl lyrics sheet says that it is called Boots 'n' Boots; someone lost their Roots I think…

Chapman hiccups while the bar-room horns lazily take us in…

Sailing on not too far 'til I get there

Chapman's voice in Americana mode again like Leroy, as the piano stomps behind him until the funk picks up, and you can see the piano guy in the smoky bar, then the chorus chips in with clearer vocals, the horns singing behind him, Whitney's acoustic guitar beautiful behind. I'm floating along with the song which is taking us back to those care free days when the world was your oyster if you wanted it to be…

Boot and roots there is so much I've got to see

Chapman hums thoughtfully, guitar and horns float then Whitney's picking guitar becomes more prominent as we go back to the story that rolls away quietly.

Banger

And here we go swing-time with a jazzy instrumental by Roger and Charlie. There is a New Orleans feel to this track driven by the sultry laid back horns and bar-room piano. The song rolls along with a memorable riff which is definitely in big band country with the hint of a western style guitar interlude which sort of highlights the overall Americana feel to the album. There is almost a strip club vibe to the music and you can imagine some exotic set of dancers moving slowly and sensually to it, setting you up perfectly for the next track which continues in a similar vein to this song as it fades…

Sweet Desiree

This song was a favourite of my school days girlfriend at the time I seem to remember and here we find Family in a slow, sultry, funky mood that is quite erotic in its own way, the lyrics igniting desires, hitting all the right spots… so that is why she liked it so much?

This song was a single and should have been another big hit for the band but what do those fickle 'popsters' know about real music?

A frantic piano opens then into the funk with Family…

Ahh, lady

You and your crazy ways

You in that negligee… Ooh saucy!

Chapman sings with backing band vocals, voices that interplay, taking different leads, the brass suddenly fluttering in while the vocalists sing together...

Sweet Desiree, come softly to me

The horns blaring now, until the piano break and Ashton sings blues style...

You got me going like a man on fire

That must be why they call you Miss Desire

And the song dances along, everyone and everything vying for attention at the end.

Suspicion

Then the funk picks up pace, drums hopping with a song that instantly makes you want to dance around like a loon, those horns cutting through you like a hot knife through butter. It should have been a single maybe? *Ah reckon so!*

Lyrically, the song is pure Chapman, offering advice about life and how you should maybe react to it, to bypass those age old suspicions...

The drumbeat is infectious, the horns on the money *Whoa!*

Said I don't make much money

But for me it's suffice

Chapman growls harmoniously, the background vocals spontaneous, the horns blaring now. Great drums by the ever brilliant Rob Townsend as a piano picks up on the funk, the horns aiding the beat...

Age old suspicion is so hard to put down

As we swirl, lost in the beat and rhythm, Chapman still growling until the piano winds the song up.

Check Out

So here we have Family's final song on the album and it is a suitable blazing rocker too, a fitting end to the album although it was not known at the time that it would be the end of an era... Check Out, how suitable a title is that?

Once again we are in that bluesy Americana as Roger Chapman sings about an escaped prisoner on the run, maybe Paul Newman in Cool Hand Luke; that is the sort of imagery you get from Chappo.

Whitney's choppy guitar sets the mood with a haunting organ behind it while the drums easily pick out the rhythm...

Since sun-up this hammer ain't been out my grip

Chapman's vocals are lush and biting at the same time as once again those now familiar horns burst in with the driving rhythm of the song. The prisoner hits the guard...

So hard I know he'll never wake
Then he's...
Over the fields and through the woods beyond
And the organ grooves as the guy runs...
Been on the run for14 days or so
And the song rock and rolls along, guitar solo high pitched in the background, piano organ wild...
It's time to check out
Well it's too late to stop now...
And they did check out and they did not stop...

Yee haw! That was one great ride, thanks for the memory guys!

Review

It's Only A Movie is a musical direction that Roger Chapman and Charlie Whitney would continue on with their following album called Streetwalkers. It's Only A Movie is a simmering cauldron or maybe a smoking coffee pot of Americana, full of Chapman and Whitney style funk that takes you back to that bygone era of the fifties, when life was simple, when going to see a movie was the highlight of the week, when all you craved was one of those American style cars, when all you wanted was some kind of a break, a new start, in a new city possibly but be careful of those Miss Desiree's and those nagging suspicions, you just might end up out of luck, somewhere you will want to check out of.

Yes, for me It's Only A Movie is a great album, just a new direction that is all, possibly instigated by the new band as Roger Chapman alludes to at the start of this chapter but Chapman and Whitney were already heading that way, two guys grooving along, running towards a new horizon.

CHAPMAN WHITNEY

STREETWALKERS
1974

So there we have it, the end of Family but not the end of the Chapman and Whitney story or of mine.

It was another bitter sweet year for me. Bitter for three reasons, I thought that I had found real love then lost it during the summer holidays, a flame that mysteriously fizzled out without any drama and for no apparent reason, something which I have mentioned in more detail in my part autobiographical sci-fi thriller novel The Wrong Reality. Bitter because my dog Bengo died, my ever faithful friend who had been with me throughout my troubled teenage years. The other bitterness came from the inevitable break up of my parent's marriage, leaving me sort of stranded and adrift at the same time.

I did stay at home for a few weeks I seem to remember then eventually my mother wanted me to move to my sister Dot's house where I would stay until moving away for my college degree. I suppose this did affect my A-level studies but I did get a Grade A in Art, the mark given for classroom coursework, my final piece being a large stand up art board cut out of Brian Eno's head with a montage of objects from the cover of his debut Here Come The Warm Jets album, all illustrated and painted by me. Like my old school Family haversack, I did still have this artwork and looking through some old art folders recently it has thankfully turned up.

My school drawing of Eno.

The second part of the marking system was a written art history exam and how I passed that is a miracle as on the eve of the exam, I had been heavily drinking Newcastle Brown Ale once again in Dickie Lincoln's house trying to study the history of architecture from a small pocket sized book while the heavy sounds of Black Sabbath blasted in the background.

My initial sketch of Chapman and Whitney for my A-Level Art Exam.
I discarded this drawing and drew a better version for the final piece.

The third part of the art mark was judged by the artistic response to a series of random titles, I chose The Inevitable Consequence and here I used a picture I had of Roger Chapman and Charlie Whitney sitting in thirties gangster style clothing at a card table. I drew Elkie Brooks as a moll girl standing beside them and in the bottom right of the picture was a hand on the floor with five fallen aces next to it. I think it was this drawing that gained me the grade A and the picture of Chapman and Whitney was a promotional interview picture for their new Streetwalkers album. I really wish that I still had that picture and obviously the artwork which was sent off to Bretton Hall in Yorkshire to be marked but was never returned, maybe they were Chapman Whitney fans and hung it on the wall there? You know, I did a year's PGTC course there and now I kick myself for not attempting to trawl through their archives, not sure if they would have kept artwork from so long ago though but I should have at least tried in my free time there, damn! Anyway, I did eventually find a picture of that photo-shoot reference (above) and it now hangs on my kitchen wall, a nice reminder of that artwork and I do now recall drawing this work on my sister's table as homework.

After a year or so, I did go back and see my father and he had managed to pull himself out of the drunken downward spiral and had even returned to work, they had kept his job open not just because he was something of a war hero but because he was damned good at his work. He still drank every day though but not in the suicidal excess of previous years. He was suddenly more approachable and talkative and I did actually go drinking with him at the club and one day my friends Mick and Steve came along too and my father gave them a lesson in how to play darts I seem to remember now ha-ha.

This was the Ford and Hylton Social working man's club in Pennywell and it always reminds me of the time I saw Paul Thompson with his girl friend in there. I have talked to Paul about this and he reckons that he was there to see a great local band called Becket whose first album strangely enough was produced by Roger Chapman. I must have been sitting on the other side of the concert room and I have a vivid memory of the compere introducing Paul saying that "we have a member of The Roxy Music in the audience tonight," Paul stood up and waved but the rough regulars of that club probably had no idea who 'The' Roxy Music was, even though I think For Your Pleasure was out and Virginia Plain had been or was about to be a massive hit for them.

It was strange however, returning to that house in Pennywell and things had disappeared, things sold maybe during my father's darker times. One such thing that was missing was my Marvel and DC comic's collection that I had collected since I was a young kid. This collection would have brought hundreds and thousands of pounds today because they were first editions in mint condition. I think my father used them to light the coal fire as like me he had no idea what their future worth would be, thousands of pounds literally going up in smoke, but that is the sort of luck me and my family have had over the years.

Back in the Sixth Form common room, like It's Only A Movie, the Chapman and Whitney Streetwalkers album was a big success with the sixth-formers, especially with the girls I seem to remember. So it brings me back to that thought that maybe it should have been Family's next album. I have to confess that the Streetwalkers band name is not a name I particularly like, a bit like Roger Chapman stating recently that he hated The Family name initially. I thought and still do that they have should kept the Chapman Whitney song-writing team brand, I think that this would have been stronger for them both commercially and critically, although they were always favourites with the music press, a great hard working down-to-earth band.

I now remember seeing the Streetwalkers at the Mayfair in Newcastle (twice there I think) and at one of the concerts there, I went to the dressing room after the gig to get autographs. The band were changing into fresh clothes and were in different stages of undress, much to the delight of my 'girlfriend' and we got a chance to speak to Chappo. That night there had been a very poor turnout and Roger asked me if I had seen any posters or press advertising and I said "no" and that I had only heard about the gig by word of mouth which really enraged Roger as the band had paid for local advertising, so it seemed that the guy responsible had taken their money but had not produced anything. I wonder if Chappo ever caught up with that guy?

Also, I think it was that night that there was a drunken troublemaker at the front of the stage and in 'these Streetwalker boots are made for booting' fashion, the guy's head was unlucky to clash with Chappo's boot as Chappo stomped wildly about with the mic-stand. The dazed guy was quickly taken backstage by a couple of roadies. When the bloodied guy eventually returned from the side of the stage, he was smiling and waved briefly and then he rejoined the crowd, he was as happy as Larry and was no further trouble. The roadies had obviously worked their magic on him.

I have constantly and faithfully followed Roger Chapman through his remarkable and illuminous career and have everything he has put out, my favourites probably being the Chappo debut album, the Live In Hamburg album and the brilliant Kiss My Soul album and now we have the excellent Life In The Pond album. I remember going to see him with my friend Mick Averre and his lovely wife Pauline at the Northumbria University in Newcastle during the 'Live In Hamburg' tour and one of the doormen saying to us, "Are you here to see that Charlie Chaplin guy?"

The Hare and Hounds probably, Roger, Gregory, Steve Park and Mackenzie.

I have waited to get Roger and the band's autographs on a few occasions and I have mentioned their music many times in my novels but I guess the most surreal moment of my life was sitting in the back of my friend Kevin Rafferty's car while Chappo sang along to one of his own songs. Roger had become friends with a good friend of mine in London called Steve Park who lived nearby and who subsequently arranged for us to pick Roger and two band members up at the Newcastle train station for a gig in South Shields. Roger sat in the front seat and I sat in the back next to Stevie Simpson and John Lingwood. Somehow Ryhope, the village that my mother was from, came into the conversation which made Stevie think of an old girlfriend he knew from Ryhope. Small world isn't it. There was a Chappo/Family compilation tape of mine in the car cassette player and when Ready For You from A Stone Unturned came on, Roger began to sing along (see, I told you that these were songs you could sing along with) and afterwards he wondered why they never played that song live and it is a fantastic song. So how unbelievably surreal was that then?

Raff drove us to the Washington Post House hotel then onto the Cellar nightclub in South Shields for the sound check. This was again getting too surreal as it seemed like this was some little private concert for us, and a reward for giving Chappo and the guys a lift and also we were given a t-shirt each. A great memory indeed and if one day I only have one memory cell left then I hope this is on it.

On the night the band was superb and Dickie Lincoln, who was not exactly a Family fan, came with us to the gig and commented on how great Roger Chapman's voice was, he had never seen him live and those old daft teenage arguments about who was the best band were now long forgotten.

Raff and Roger, not the Cellar, somewhere in Peterlee, Kick It Back Tour.

After the Great North Run, me and Dickie Lincoln (right)

Another fond memory, one of many I should add, is of Roger's concert at the The Park Hotel in Tynemouth on the 21st December 1998. Steve and I took our young families to the concert and that was the night I caught one of Roger's drumsticks at the front and like an idiot, I gave it to a woman who was standing next to me who had asked for it and I am pretty sure that she said "idiot" instead of thanks, so any chance of giving that drumstick back to me now? Ha-ha.

College days, Steve Nanson (left) and me, (V-neck sweaters are cool.)

Also, after the concert we went for a drink in the bar and Roger and the band were sitting at a table, all of our kids, Carl, James, Mathew and Rachel went up to the table and asked Roger to sing Habits Of A Lifetime again and he signed my son's water bottle and a beer mat for Mathew. My friend Steve gave Chappo one of those funny smelling cigarettes as a thank you.

These days I am an admin for the Family with Roger Chapman Appreciation Society Facebook page and I have to say that it is an honour and a privilege, our numbers doubling and increasing day by day which proves that Family are definitely not forgotten.

With the help of Trevor Gardiner, I recently managed to organise Questions & Answers with Roger and here are his answers to member's questions from three Facebook groups.

CHAPPO EXCLUSIVE! - Thanks again to Trevor Gardiner, thanks to those that participated and of course, many thanks to Roger Chapman himself.

Questions for Roger Chapman...

FAMILY WITH ROGER CHAPMAN APPRECIATION SOCIETY

Mick St Michael - What moment in your musical history would you like to revisit, either to savour or to change?
RC - FIRST TOUR USA.

Richard Valanga - What do you think is your greatest achievement?
RC - ACHIEVEMENT: OH GOD SO MANY
MAYBE JERRY LEE LEWIS RECORDING "BIG ROLL DADDY"
OR MAYBE GEORGIE FAME ASKING ME TO START A BAND WITH HIM.
OR MAYBE BEING ASKED TO FRONT THE BB KING BAND.

What do you consider to be your greatest song?
RC - SONG: PROBABLY "THE WEAVERS ANSWER"
OR MAYBE "ALL TOO SOON" OR MAYBE "NO MULES FOOL" OR SUMMAT ELSE.

Paul Bamford -Happy Birthday! Have you got any jelly and ice cream left?!!
RC - NO BUT GOT LOADSA STRAWBERRY TEQUILAS.

David Dicker - Do you remember the Van Dike club Devonport?
RC - AHH THE DICK VAN DICK CLUB. SHOULDN'T THAT BE DYKE?

Dave Jeanes - Why is Red Card so under-rated? Great songs on there; lyrically and musically.
RC- FEEBLE MINDED PUBLIC I SUPPOSE DAVE, IT'S ALWAYS THEIR FAULT.

Kev Mellotron- Any chance of Playing The Robin Bilston again, if so can we buy you a drink?
RC - BE QUICKER IF YOU SEND IT BY AMAZON

Dave Mackenzie -Why do you give Twiggy such a hard time?
RC - COZ HES A PRATT.

Shirley Powell - Does your favourite track vary dependant on your mood.
...do you even have one?
RC - HI SHIRL, IV'E GOT ONE NOW 🖤🖤🩶🩶
Shirley Powell - Good thing about Family is - all our moods are in there...

HI SHIRL ETC ETC ETC

Suzzy Mcdonnell - Bay Hotel Sunderland Maggie and me xx
YES I REMEMBER IT WELL, LOVELY PLACE AND OF COURSE YOU AND
MAGGIE

Peter Hall - Hi Rog, You have always surrounded your bands with
outstanding musicians! Question which band would you have fancied
being in? Happy belated birthday
RC - TA PETE. SEX PISTOLS, I'D AVE GIVE ROTTEN A RUN FOR HIS MONEY

Terry Edwards - Roger played bass on a John Peel session, alto sax on
MIADH, he is pictured with a guitar on A Turn Unstoned, what other
instruments does Roger play?
RC – I'LL ASK HIM.

ROGER CHAPMAN PAGE

Judy Allen - I first discovered Family in 1967 when I was 13; I loved
nearly every track, which was one of your favourites?
RC - TOO MANY TO COUNT JUDY BUT SUNS UP THERE.

Bruce Morrison Kirk - What do you like most about being from
Leicestershire?
RC - BEING A FOX.

Jon Hounsome - Was the shadow on the wall your shadow?
RC - AS FAR AS MIKE WENT YES.

Sandie Smith - When you next heading to the North East?
RC - SOON AS POSS SAN.

Karola Recke - Do you still have memories of your catering team Charlie & Moni in Germany, in the 90 years?
RC - CERTAINLY DO KAZ

Dave Needham - Are there any major decisions you made in your career you would change with hindsight, what would it or they be?
RC - POXY THIEVING MANAGERS.

UK ROCK GROUP FAMILY FANS

Paul Barnett - I would like to ask Roger - who were your musical influences?
RC - ELVIS BUT ILL NEVER REPLACE HIM

Mark Ewels - I would like to ask Roger.... what can we expect from your new album and did you enjoy making it?
RC - DIFFERENT FEEL NEW SONGS AND YES DIFFERENT IN LOCKDOWN.

Charles Douglas - Just too young to catch Family live; saw Streetwalkers many times and they were always superb. Charlie Whitney is so underrated and hardly ever mentioned along with the usual suspects of that time. Is he ok and could we possibly see him together with you in the future? And thanks for the great music over the years.
RC - YOURE WELCOME CHARLIE

Col Patterson - I would like to ask Roger, when can we expect you're autobiography. You have given us over 50 years of amazing music; you must have so many great stories to tell?
RC - OH YOU ARE NAUGHTY COL!

Dermot Mitchell - Does he have bad memories of Streetwalkers? He was asked about them at the time of the Family reunion eight years or so ago and replied emphatically that they would not be reforming.
RC - I HAVE BAD MEMORIES OF ALL DERMOT BUT YOU AIN'T HEARING EM.

Fred Weyerman - What's the toughest mic stand he's ever had a go at, and who won?

RC - MIKE WON FRED AND THERE ARE PICS TO PROVE IT.

Craig Cassidy - I'd love to learn about Roger's recollections of the co-writing process with Charlie - i.e., did chord changes precede lyrics? Was it two men in a room banging it out? How did it evolve over time? How intentional were the different sounds/styles of each Lp? What unique strengths did each of them bring to the writing partnership?! (And Happy Day, Dude!!)
RC - WELL IT CERTAINLY WASN'T TWO MEN BANGING IT ABOUT IN A ROOM CRAIG BUT THANX FOR THE MEMORY

Thomas Coldwater Man - I want to ask Roger: In two comments to a birthday post of Roland Holroyd I added two private pictures with you and me and forgot to ask you for permission. I know to ask after I did it is someway stupid but to calm my soul I would like to know what you think about it. And if a second question is ok: Are there any plans for you to come back again to Germany in the future? We all would love to see you one more/last time...!
RC - I HAVE NO IDEA ON THE PIC YOU'RE TALKING ABOUT TOM BUT I'D LIKE TO THINK I'LL BE PROMOTING "LIFE IN THE POND" EVERYWHERE. MAYBE A VIDEO WILL DO IT.

Alan Roberts - I would like to know if Roger is sincere about answering some very emotive genuine questions. Will he be able to answer them all personally?? Cos I have a very meaningful longish question for him regarding my love of his music, voice, and my 45 year plight of trying to see him live. I have failed thru bad luck to come from Australia 3 times and missed him, I have converted 100s of MUSOS here. Some like myself. Do Family. Short list. Mostly Streetwalkers n Chappo.. Yet I'm frustrated in the fear of never seeing a man who has been a massive influence and a pleasure in my 74 yrs. X
RC - OZZY OZZY OZZY OZ LOVE IT, WENT THERE ON HOLIDAY 15 YEARS AGO. ONLY PLACE I'VE EVER BEEN AND WANTED TO STAY. SAY HELLO TO BARNSEY HE'S A PAL O MINE AS WELL.

Thanks again for Roger's participation in this Q&A.

To wind up this memoir then, I would like to finish with Roger's new release, Life In The Pond which is getting rave reviews from both press and fans alike, Roger proving that there is life in 'The Guv' still. The music is great, the voice still vital and powerful. There is probably more of a blues rock feel to this album, which I like as I am still a massive fan

of blues music. The album is a Chapman/Palmer production and of course Poli Palmer is quite unbelievably superb as the only other musician is the excellent guitarist Geoff Whitehorn on three of the tracks.

More please guys.

Below is just one of the many glowing reviews of Life In The Pond and many thanks to Ian D Hall of Liverpool Sound and Vision for his most excellent review of the album and his permission to show it here.

Life In The Pond Review
Liverpool Sound and Vision Rating 8.5/10

There was once a school of thought, typified by the reaction of the old-fashioned critic, that those who are prolific in their writing are not as dedicated to their craft as those who can take years to produce a single piece of art. It is of course rubbish, a nonsense that is insult to the creativity of a human being when they are touched by the continued navigation of the Muse.

An example of such comes in the form to which Kerouac was subject to ridicule when people found out he wrote his seminal novel, On The Road in three weeks, but it was described and decried as 'Barbaric Yawp', and even Truman Capote criticised Kerouac's style, saying "That it wasn't writing, it's typing". Whether it is on the road, or the visual scene captured in Life In The Pond, the prolific are just as just as important to framing existence as their steady beat counterparts.

It is when the two states of appreciation clash, that is when there are fireworks, beautiful, enticing, shocking, the slam dunk of cautious optimism meeting heroic cool; and despite the grace of Roger Chapman not figuring in the studio for some time, he nevertheless has been continuous in his output, his mind working overtime and bleeding words and notes as if they were water running over smoothed down pebbles and into the mere, scattering the fish of panic into the darkest, unfathomable depths.

Often cited as the voice of his generation, Roger Chapman takes that continuous writing ethic and returns with a new album, Life In The Pond, and joins the seams together after seven decades of being one of the most considerate, consummate and completed artists to be found, and Life In The Pond continues that sense of unmatched persuasion with aplomb.

Through tracks such as the opener Dark Side Of The Stairs, Rabbit Got The Gun, Having Us A Honey Moon, On Lavender Heights and Green As Guacamole, Roger Chapman reaffirms his place as one of Britain's deep reflective thinkers and lyric and music writers; and it is one that puts a line under the absence from the studio with delicate ease.

To perhaps liken the genial sense of harmony of Roger Chapman with the poetic beat of Kerouac might seem as though it is a marriage of convenience, however the world has turned to a point where the observations of one man who left us over half a century ago, is reflected in the examination of another, very much keeping the pen scribing away. A welcome return doesn't quite have the gravitas of meaning, for Life In The Pond is the great continuance of a master in his prime.

Ian D Hall, Liverpool Sound and Vision.

These are observations from a...

Recently I thought that it would be cool to invite Family fans to comment on one of their favourite bands and to include their responses in this updated edition so a big thank you to all that participated.

ROGER CHAPMAN'S VOICE

Richard Valanga
A powerful creative psychedelic blues voice that is full of soul and inner feeling, completely unique and individual, it is a voice that can rock like no other yet can be so beautifully laid back, cool and mellow when needed. Roger's voice really is an original work of art!

Steven Maginnis
Bleating terror.

Peter Graves
Unique
Loved the band from first time I heard "Scene though the eye of a lens."

Dave Mackenzie
Pure emotion.

Skip Felts
Impassioned warbling.

Colin Fraser

Powerful. Soulful. Rocking. Jazz. Quite simply the best vocalist you will ever hear .

Alex Scrivener
Larry the Lamb, sir! Known to all as " A right Herbert".

Paul Tropman
Awesome. I remember hearing him live singing Kiss My Soul at the Robin Hood in Dudley. Yeah, just awesome!

Dave Brown
My late sister gave me Music in a Dolls House for my birthday in 1970. In my card she wrote 'if this album doesn't open your mind to progressive music, nothing will" After one listen, I was hooked, and over 50 years later, still am.

Rab Sneddon
A man who gargles with rusty nails.

Nigel Smith
I remember at 15 seeing Family at Southsea, blew my mind Chappo played a sax,great vocalist. Thank you love Chappo and Family.

Peter Hall
Original and unforgettable.

Gene Grimes
A baritone banshee.

Carole Johnson
From the soul.

Chris Flood
Girgling.

David Lightfoot
Gravel crunching.

James Johnson

A voice with honey coated gravel !

James Johnson
Legend!

Harry Conlon
Cannot be compared to anyone and is a brilliant origina.l

Paul Copley
A breath of fresh air.

Rose Prentice
The most amazing voice, I was shaking with emotion at Woburn... so exiting!

Merlina Waterworth
A unique expression of raw emotion. A black singer in a white skin.
David Lightfoot
Merlina Waterworth that's a very good comment, as Ray Charles was one his heroes
Merlina Waterworth
David Lightfoot, yes, along with other black artists such as The Coasters. Plus the one other place I've heard that warble in vocals is with some African singers.
In the eighties I filmed a performance by South African jazz musician Dudu Pukwana, who played saxophone but his presence and energy reminded me of Chappo.
I think especially as he's got older it's apparent he's very much rooted in the traditions of jazz and blues. The guitarist who used to play with Dudu, Lucky Ranku, ended up teaching guitar to white kids, and he said the thing they were often missing was the ability to really feel the music. But Chappo has always had that, which he probably absorbed from Ray Charles and other black artists.
Tom Roach
Like Peyton Park...
Merlina Waterworth
Tom Roach - Great track - never heard of 'em! But definitely in the same vein. Can imagine Chappo doing a great cover of this track!
Tom Roach
Merlina Waterworth, yes I can.

Peyton E. Park was a Dallas Texas singer, musician and actor. He was also an old friend and neighbor of my father and Dad used to tell me that Ray Charles got his singing style from Peyton. I kind of didn't believe him until I read that Ray Charles had come to Dallas to "find his voice", so perhaps he did?

Merlina Waterworth

I wonder if Roger is aware of Peyton Park? I'm sure he would be interested to know who influenced Ray Charles....and Chappo is part of that lineage!

Richard Valanga I think you should definitely mention this in your update. I belief Life in the Pond was in part a tribute to jazz and blues artists from the past, from listening to Jazz FM.

I sent Rog an email at the start of lockdown, I think at the time of sending birthday greetings, mentioning that I was currently listening to Classic FM and learning about the lives of classical composers.

Maybe that's what gave him the idea to listen to Jazz FM and learn more about the history of the genre of music that has influenced and inspired him.

One other connection is that Lucky Ranku's band Jabula feature on Mike Oldfield's albums Omnadawn and (I think) Incantations, providing the African drumming. And Chappo of course has also worked with Mike Oldfield, who once auditioned to join Family.

I was also inspired to write an original song about Chappo after learning the chords to Between Blue and Me at a local 'rock school', and combined it with one of Dudu Pukwanas tracks as a kind of medley.

I put it on a cassette and Lucky Ranku listened to it and thought that it did fit with Dudu's number, and envisaged adding some 'horns' to it.

A bit of a tangent, but it does further illustrate the connection between the music of Chappo and Family and the tradition of Jazz and Blues and it's African origins.

Merlina Waterworth

One other African connection is one of my favorite tracks from his solo career, The Drum. It was explained to me at one point by Lucky Ranku's uncle Dan who I knew, how the drums within the African tradition are the way of calling the tribe to come together. And Chappo's The Drum reflects that.

Nick Coltman

Sounds Like Joe Cocker who has swallowed Broken Glass. Superb, I Just keep Rollin and Tumblin Lardy.

Jake Janulevicius
His voice is unique and I love it.

Lawrence Flusk
What is time within my mind is a red rose red to a man who is blind. Where do I look for truth what do I see as I sail on my voyage of truth . With lyrics like this delivered by a voice like his is heaven. So yes a voice made in Heaven in the Iron furnace.

Neil Cobbett
Chapman and Whitney sound once described as "Bombsite vocals and sledgehammer guitar" (obviously the latter courtesy of Charlie!)

Kev Mellotron
Soulful... Gutsy... Passionate... Just The Best!

Judy Allen
His voice is unique!

Jamie Martinez
Chappo is God!

CHARLIE WHITNEY'S GUITAR PLAYING

Richard Valanga.
THE Riff King, powerhouse chords like no other and his style was unique and original, always just right for the song. Totally individual and beautifully sensitive when needed, one the great rock guitarists of all time.

William R. Heideman
Intricately Powerful!

Martin Wilkinson
Strange but wonderful, I don't think people understand how original this guy's playing was. Marvellous.

Dave Jeanes
Second to none.

Roberto Fronzi
Strangely underrated.

Neil Cobbett
Charlie was a powerful player but considerably more subtle than a lot of the "heavy brigade". Being a really good songwriter didn't hurt any either. One of the few over here who got the West Coast feel.

Alan Givens
Understated and underrated.

Rich Barton
Unique.

Pete Linton
Supremely tasteful.

Nigel Smith
Clever underrated.

Richard Parker
Original, tasteful, creative. He played exactly what the song needed and never overplayed.

Pam Chritchlow
When I first heard him in Tony Bart and the Revels back in the early 60's, I thought he was amazing, he made his guitar sing and was always true to the original songs.

Terry Cowlishaw
I agree with you, Pam. I used to go with Harry Ovenall to rehearsals at the back of the pub in Great Glen. I thought it was amazing, especially with Tony doing his Cliff Rock'n' Roll stuff. But of course there was much more to Johnnie's playing (I never knew him as 'Charlie') and they used to do some pretty smart instrumentals too. I was chuffed to bits to do a gig with them much later at the Art College.

Pam Chritchlow

Terry Cowlishaw I fell in love with Tony's 'Cliff' and Harry's drum solo!!!!
I too only knew 'Charlie' as Johnny!!!!
Was Harry's solo 'Let there be drums'?
We used to love jiving faster and faster to his amazing drum solo!!!! X
If I remember correctly, Pam, Harry's solo was in a Shadows number,
either 'See You in My Drums' or 'Shadoogie'. I'll have to ask him
Pam Chritchlow
Terry Cowlishaw I will look them up and have a listen. X

Kev Mellotron
Original.

Dave Maddock-Brown
Well tasty.

Jim dela Piedra
One of my favorites.

Johnny Har
One of my favorites, Elements of Rock, Jazz, Prog, Blues, Country.

Alain Celos
Underrated !

Steven Maginnis - Admin.
He sprays notes from his guitar like bullets from a machine gun.

Laurence Collins
Brilliant, he's a stunne.r

David Parker
Don't forget his part in the Whitney/Chapman song-writing team.

Colin Ward
his playing and Rogers unusual voice is what gave Family their sound.

Dave Mackenzie
Eclectic.

Kenneth Nessing

Incredibly clever and melodic.

Mathew Underwood
Incisive.

Tom Recchion
Unparalleled and inventive.

Chris Cantor
More rhythm than lead orientated.

Alain Cado
Beatlesque... "The Glove
Neil Cobbett
Alain Cado He really liked George Harrison's playing and song-writing
Neil Cobbett
When Ken and Poli left the band he rejigged it even more in the style of
the Beatles.

Pete Robinson
His attack and phrasing was like no other. He could construct a melodic
and biting solo but always in the service of the song.

Dave Stewart
Admirable.

Raymond Bailey
Great to listen too, that's what matters to me.

Kevin McCormick
He was good in his own way.

Steve Samuels
Quirky, melodic, inventive, unpredictable, oriental.

Stuart Ragland
Always appropriate, with the most satisfying tones and textures, of
which I have long been envious. Like a handful of players, including Peter
Green and David Gilmour, he did not have to rely on playing fast. He just
played the right notes at the right time. He must have just loved hearing

them go by as they complemented everything else that was happening in the songs.

Ken Hornsby
Bit avant-garde.

Dave Dodo-bones
Dynamite!

Alan Roberts
His very own. An individual, simple as that.

Steve Ball
Amazing.

Colin Fraser
Just listen to the guitar solo on glove... I rest my case.
Stuart Ragland
Try working it out on guitar. It is a wonderful lesson in melodic playing and in how to go from high to low at the beginning, and then how to work your way up the neck through various chord inversions, and then end the solo by resolving on a low note.

SY'n'KRO
Totally Unique & Truly Wonderful. He created that "Family Sound".

Garry Norris
Underatted

Neil Cobbett
More than even Chapman, Charlie was Family.

Ian Clarke
Unique and versatile, so many influences can be detected but it always came out as original.

Dave Needham
Very much underrated.

Janiou Fleco

Complimentary to Chappo.

Robert Gray
Exactly what's needed for the gig.

Robert Plosky
Different.

Luc Van Goethem
Quite easy, a very underestimated guitar player.

Dave Mackenzie
Idiosyncratic.

Eddy Collins
Amazing.

MEMORIES

Dominic Ferns
I saw Family play twice in the late sixties once at the Town Hall Torquay and once at the Philharmonic Hall Liverpool very unique band. And what the hell bad eggs don't smell...

Lawrence Flusk
Dominic Ferns, yes also the stadium when we seen them there America the band opened for Family. Horse with no name the song that became very popular at the time . Also Torquay about 72 also Bickershaw music festival . Also at least another few times in various other places always great like you Dom.

Laur Inness
I remember seeing chapman and Whitney streetwalkers, at the Valley, on the May Bank Holiday, 1st on the bill. I thought they were great. On the Friday following, I walked into the Mayfair, Newcastle-upon-Tyne and who should be standing there, but Chappo and Bobby Tench, I went over had a nice chat and drink with two really nice people, they explained they were not happy about the P.A system they had used at Charlton, but I would never have known. Made my night.

Richard Rhodes

I knew the band well and went to the finale party at the Holiday Inn Leicester ...Chappo came to my first wedding. He also came to my country cottage with America. I also went on holiday with the band to Tunisia where they played a memorable gig at Club Med.

Michael Carroll

About 20 years ago I was working at the ExCel Centre in London and decided to take a day off to drive to Southampton to see Chappo at The Brook. I arrived at the venue around 4.30pm. Outside was Henry Spinetti who was the drummer for The Shortlist at that time. He was very friendly and we chatted for a while. He then invited me into the sound check. The band were very nice because they recognised me from previous gigs I'd attended. Steve Simpson sat and told me how he'd built his white "Frankencaster" from other guitars - a trick Clapton has practised on occasions. Around 6pm, the road manager approached me and asked if I had a car. I said yes, and he then asked if I'd give Roger a lift to the Highfield Hotel so that he could have a pre-gig nap. On the way to the hotel, Roger asked me where I was from and was intrigued when I told him I was from Hinckley - a town near Leicester. This wasn't quite right, but my home town of Atherstone is very close and I wasn't sure whether Roger would have heard of it. After dropping him off, I went back to The Brook and informed the road manager that my "special package" had been delivered safely. That night, after the gig, I returned to my hotel in Goodmayes, East London. On the way, I stopped at a motorway services for a toilet break. A car followed me into the parking area and pulled up next to mine. Out stepped the late Ian Gibbons, The Shortlist's keyboard player, who told me he was on his way back home to Southend. Since we had both stopped for the same reason there was nothing else for it. We entered the toilets and happily emptied our bladders in stereo. Having dispelled our urinary discomfort, Ian then followed me back to East London where we split our mini convoy at the A13. He went East, I went West. I got back to my hotel about 2am. It had been a good day.

Michael Walsh

Living in the States, I did not have a chance to see Family much. The first time I had a chance was the Elton John tour. We hit a tremendous traffic jam and by the time we got to the show Family was on. I swear to god, I

was there for 30 seconds and they finished the song they were playing and said, "Good night, Philly! I had 3rd row seats and left! Elton is okay, but I was not there to see him.I had to come over to England to see "Family reunion" at Shepherd's Bush. Not really Family but as close as I was gonna come. I look forward to reading your memoir!
I have to support Family Fans!

Bruce Wright
We firstly got to see them in late 69, 20 years of age, so much amazing music, groups, at this time, too many to mention, bar this one Family, they overwhelmed us, 53 years on, stills hits the spot.
Fills me up with such memories, cheers B.

Jeff Gifford
Reading Material for the trip Pt.3 - The Music Of Family And Me A Memoir.
My friend, writer Richard Valanga assimilated his thoughts in an album by album, song by song memoir of his favorite band British Prog band Family. To my American friends: Don't feel in the dark when it comes to this band and the fact you have never heard, let alone heard OF Family. I'm talking to folks my age when I say this. It's a pretty sure bet no one you know has heard of them either. Folks my age from Great Britain and Europe need no introduction in most cases.

I have many of the bands albums on vinyl or cd and reading Richard's book is like sitting down and listening to one of my all time favorite bands with a friend.

Thanks Richard, this is a beaut.

AND FINALLY…

Oh and before I finish this memoir, I thought that I would tell you about what happened to that first Family t-shirt of mine. My sister Dot did not have a sewing machine any more so I decided to frame the remaining image and I also breathed new life into it by amending the artwork and having it printed onto a new t-shirt. Family and Chappo will live forever.

Richard Valanga -
3.20pm, The Alamo, Washington, 22/7/2021.

Framed... and a old t-shirt new t-shirt.

Kitchen poster – Kick It Back Tour.

Some of my concert tickets from recent times.

THE GUILDHALL
PORTSMOUTH

ADMIT AT

John and Tony Smith

present

THE FAMILY

IN CONCERT

Tuesday, 16th November

at 7.30 p.m.

STALLS

NORTH
EAST
DOOR

ROW

C

SEAT

19

85p

TO BE RETAINED

TICKETS CANNOT
BE EXCHANGED OR
MONEY REFUNDED

ACME PRINTING CO., LTD., PORTSMOUTH

One of Trev's tickets. Picture courtesy of Trevor Gardiner.

ACKNOWLEDGEMENTS

The amazing lyrics of Roger Chapman; and many thanks for the feedback and use of your personal pictures Roger.
Many thanks to Trevor Gardiner, advice, project help and ticket picture.
Simon Boxall, feedback and advice.
Paul Thompson, Roxy Music - Music In A Doll's House comment.
Ian D Hall, Liverpool Sound and Vision.
Del Gentleman, John Mulvey and Jim Irvin - Mojo Magazine.
Roger Smith - http://www.readysteadygone.co.uk/geoff-docherty/
The Eric Clapton fan - Marc Andelane.

1   - Sgt. Pepper Lonely Hearts Club Band, The Beatles.
2   - In The Court Of The Crimson King, King Crimson.
3   - Led Zeppelin 2, Led Zeppelin.
4   - The Bay Hotel, Seaburn, Sunderland.
5   - John Lennon.
6   - Music In A Doll's House album design by Peter Duval.
7   - Music In A Doll's House front cover photography by Julian Cottrell.
8   - Music In A Doll's House back cover photography by Jac Remise.
9   - Chucky the horror movie.
10 - Entertainment album design by Alan Aldridge.
11 - Entertainment photographs for the front and back by Rodger Phillips.
12 - A Song For Me album photographer, Bill Holden.
13 - A Song For Me engineer, George Chkiantz.
14 - A Song For Me 2nd engineers, Dave Bridges, Roger Beale, Keith Harwood.
15 - Mortars with Exploding Projectiles by Leonardo da Vinci.
16 - The Velvet Underground's banana cover by Andy Warhol.
17 - The Beatle's Sgt. Peppers cover by Peter Blake.
18 - Geoff Docherty, A Promoter's Tale.
19 - Photograph of The Bay Hotel courtesy of Roger Smith.
20 - Old Songs New Songs album design by Stuart Weston.
21 - John Peel, Playhouse Theatre 16th December 1971.
22 - Fearless album cover design by John Kosh.
23 - Family Fearless cd issue/Roger Chapman quote - Mystic Records.
24 - Fearless engineer, George Chkiantz.
25 - Bandstand album cover design by John Kosh.
26 - Bandstand photography by Peter Howe.

27 - It's Only A Movie album cover design by John Kosh.
28 - It's Only A Movie engineers, George Chkiantz, John Middleton and Rod.
29 - Chapman Whitney Streetwalkers album photography by Tony Evans, cover prepared by John Kosh.
30 - Miss Dunn, Art Teacher, Pennywell School.
31 - John Peace, Artist and Art Tutor, Sunderland Art College.
32 - Jethro Tull Lend Me Your Ears book, Richard Houghton.
33 - Cherry Red Records/Esoteric Records.

Artwork By Me

Roger Says Bollocks - Charcoal pencil.

Chappo In Motion - Coloured pencils.

Chappo Good News Bad News - Abstract Digital Art - Full colour

Other books by Richard Valanga
REVIEWS

RICHARDVALANGA
THE SUNDERLAND VAMPIRE

Late at night, a man awakes in a Sunderland cemetery and is confused and alone. The man cannot remember what has happened and has no recollection of the events that have led him to such a cold and desolate place. Why was he there and more importantly... who was he?

It is not just his loss of memory that is worrying him though, it is the strange new urges that are calling to him from the surrounding darkness, unnatural thoughts that seem somehow familiar... and disturbing.

The Sunderland Vampire is a psychological paranormal mystery thriller and a ghostly gothic romance that ultimately leads back to the coastal town of Whitby.

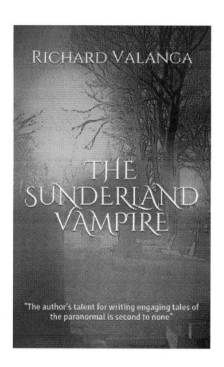

'It oozes Anne Rice...'

'A great book! Loved it.'

'This is brilliant, wonderfully vivid, very detailed and sumptuous and a pleasure to read.'

RICHARDVALANGA
THE WRONG REALITY

Running to save the life of his son, Ryan Walker and the Reverend Daniel McGovern are transported to another reality by an enigmatic blue ripple that suddenly appears on the Tyne Bridge.

For Walker, this reality provides everything he has ever desired except for the complications caused by the death of his ex-wife.

For the Reverend, the other reality is absolute Hell, a Hell that is tearing his vulnerable soul apart.

Murder, blackmail, dark eroticism and a dangerous religion threaten the sanity of the two men but there is a way back to their own reality, a possible window of opportunity that could enable them to return...

The problem is; will they realise this in time as both men are slowly being consumed by their alternate personalities.

'The author's talent for writing engaging tales of the paranormal is second to none.'

'The Wrong Reality for the real world...'
'Richard Valanga's **talented and imaginative** writing style is so suited to the supernatural genre and this together with a mix of horror and dark eroticism, **"The Wrong Reality" is proof of his superb eclectic ability to engage his readers in a truly alternative world.'**

RICHARDVALANGA
COLOSSEUM

In the theatre of death only evil reigns supreme.
During the Festival of Death in Rome, four American art students go missing. One of the students is eventually found dead, horribly mutilated as if by wild beasts inside the Colosseum.

One year later, Nick Thorn is sent by the New Sanctuary to help the father of one of the missing students, a desperate man who is still looking for his daughter.

The New Sanctuary believes that Thorn has a psychic ability, a 'special gift' that could help him; Thorn however has always denied such a thing, claiming it to be pure nonsense and probably the product of an overactive imagination instigated by his drinking problem.

Shortly after Thorn arrives in Rome, the Festival of Death begins again and another of the missing students is gruesomely murdered. It is now a race against time to find the other two.

Can Thorn find and save the remaining two students or will Mania the Roman Goddess of Death succeed in devouring their souls and satisfy the blood lust of her followers?

"The author's talent for writing engaging tales of the paranormal is second to none"

richardValanga

colosseum

the return of a forgotten evil

"Valanga writes about the Afterlife like nobody else today"

Another five star novel from Sunderland born writer...

Whenever you pick up Sunderland born Richard Valanga's novels, you just know it's going to be **filled with his most vivid imaginations and his incredibly engaging storylines,** for which he has put his heart and soul into writing them.

His latest publication "Colosseum" is no exception, this time with a visit to the chilling and haunting atmospheric location of Rome.

"In the theatre of death only evil reigns supreme. During the Festival of Death in Rome, four American art students go missing. One of the students is eventually found dead, horribly mutilated as if by wild beasts inside the Colosseum. One year later, Nick Thorn is sent by the New

Sanctuary to help the father of one of the missing students, a desperate man who is still looking for his daughter. The New Sanctuary believes that Thorn has a psychic ability, a 'special gift' that could help him. However, shortly after Thorn arrives in Rome, the Festival of Death begins again and another of the missing students is gruesomely murdered. It is now a race against time to find the other two. Can Thorn find and save the remaining two students or will Mania the Roman Goddess of Death succeed in devouring their souls and satisfy the blood lust of her followers?"

This story is quite blood thirsty, as you'd expect from the ancient gladiator days. The author has included some really spectacular graphic scenes during the Festival of Death, that really set the scene for the plot. I particularly liked the first person narrative from Nick, I found him a curious protagonist, hard drinking, heavy smoking, Robert Mitchum lookalike with a sardonic humour and a similarity to the detective Philip Marlowe and his fellow American dime heroes. His special ability with his physic dreamlike visions make him quite remarkable and the perfect detective to help find the missing students.

There is no denying Richard Valanga's talent for paranormal and horror thriller writing. His visions just keep getting stronger and stronger. "Colosseum" is his most commercial outing to date following on from some very personal and emotive novels and he's a writer I'm more than happy to continue to follow, in the future.

Excellent gripping novel   - Amazon Review 26/11/2020

Great thriller!
When a number of students go missing in Rome and one of them is later found dead in the Colosseum, a man with supposed psychic abilities is sent to investigate what happened to the missing students.

He arrives just before the Festival of Death and when another of the missing students is discovered dead in a grisly manner, tension mounts. The race is on to find and rescue the other two students, assuming they're still alive. Were they kidnapped and killed by a secret Roman cult, and tortured by a sinister group of evildoers?
This is an excellent international thriller. Gripping and suspenseful.
Highly recommended!

Stephen King meets James Herbert? Or Edgar Allen Poe.

Wow! What a story! Stephen King meets James Herbert! Maybe! A psychological tale with enough gore and horror to scare the living daylights out of you, yet **a plot to tease and intrigue you**, and characters you grow to really care about! **Well written, and excellently plotted**, this book cruises along at breakneck speed. Easy to read, very difficult to put down. **Highly recommended for those wanting a gripping, exciting story that stays with you**. This book needs a follow up ...

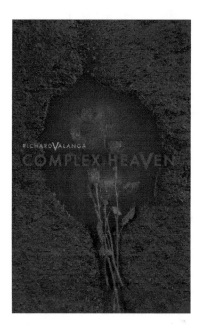

RICHARDVALANGA
COMPLEX HEAVEN

Set in the North East of England, Complex Heaven is a psychological supernatural thriller that tells the story of a troubled soul tormented by the anguish of his distraught son. Called back from the Afterlife, father of two Richard; is concerned about the mental welfare of his youngest son JJ. There is a suspicion that somehow JJ is connected to the death of a young girl called Rose in Washington. The mystery however, is much more complicated as Richard finally confronts the evil that has been preying on his family for generations. A suffering that forces Richard back to the world of the living; where the answers to some of the darkest moments of his life are waiting.

'Complex and gripping.'

RICHARD VALANGA
COMPLEX HELL

'It's present-day Sunderland and a mysterious manuscript is discovered in the house of an evil spirit, leading the unwary reader to a tale of the sixties in North East England, where not everything is quite as it seems. Forbidden love, loss and a lifetime of pure evil lie in store for whoever dares turn the ageing pages further. In Devils Wood House the memory of the missing girl, Rose, waits desperately. Unfortunately for her, time is not on her side. Can her soul be saved or will the child be lost forever?'

"Richard Valanga writes about the Afterlife like nobody else today, he's the 21st-century Dante of the North." - Tony Barrell, The Sunday Times

'Unique and interesting, thought-provoking, original and creative, it certainly is a tale that will stay in my mind.'

'Creepy paranormal read.'
'The author has a **wonderful and unique writing style** that draws you in instantly. "Complex Hell" is a wholly original take on the afterlife and quite believable too.'

'The author Richard Valanga writes like a poet and has a brilliant and impressive imagination to match.'

'A good read, good memories and pretty good musical taste...
Once again Richard **Valanga excels in not only scaring the reader to death, but evokes fond memories of a time when things were simpler,** when mobile phones and computers were still in the imagination of Science Fiction writers! I feel sure Mr Valanga actually uses the typewriter mentioned in the first chapter! A good read; good memories

and pretty good musical taste for something undead. **Richard writes like a man possessed**...because I think he probably is!'

'**A very good read.**'
'This book was **a very good read, great concept**. Scary, but engaging; I **was compelled to keep reading.**'

RICHARDVALANGA
COMPLEX SHADOWS

Fleeing Devils Wood House in Washington with a car full of ill-gotten riches; a father and his son check into the Seaburn Hotel on the Sunderland coast.

With them is the father's old manuscript which is his account of what he experienced in the jungles of Burma during World War Two. Where there is war there is immense evil, a breeding ground for dark supernatural forces that once encountered will change your life forever.

This book is the third in the Complex Series and helps explain why one family becomes entangled with and haunted by the malevolent Dark Conscious.

'A great read!!'

'I really enjoyed reading this creepy, ghostly and at times scary book. You could truly feel how passionate the author was about his personal and emotional memories during the first half of the story. The whole storyline comes together flawlessly at the end and was certainly quite emotional. **Richard Valanga is a highly talented and imaginative author and I highly recommend this wholly original book**.....it really is a frightening thought that the dead do walk our streets!!'

'Richard Valanga's amazing book Complex Shadows is not for the weak- hearted.'

'The past can be intense and in this supernatural and extremely dark thriller that takes place in the north east of England (Sunderland to be exact) he adds more to this 'one of a kind' read that will have you captive from the start with great visions of the harshness and ugly events of Burma during World War Two to the Shadows of the Past which most of us can relate to.

The attention to detail in this fine piece of work sets this apart from a lot of supernatural and paranormal books I have read. If I was a betting man and with an outstanding Hollywood agent, **I could see this on the silver screen** with an outstanding soundtrack that will draw you into this fabulous read.'

RICHARDVALANGA
COMPLEX REALITY

This is the story of one family's unfortunate entanglement with the malicious evil force known as the Dark Conscious.

A paranormal journey that takes you from present day Sunderland back to the sixties and then even further back to the World War Two jungles of Burma and the horrific beginnings of the story.

Can this persistent deadly evil be defeated, can the reborn spirits of a man and his father finally triumph over the darkness that threatens them and achieve everlasting peace for their family?

"**Richard Valanga writes about the Afterlife like nobody else today, he's the 21st – century Dante of the North.**"
- **Tony Barrell, The Sunday Times.**

A Great Read!
'**A unique and intriguing supernatural tale that blends fact and fiction and leaves the reader questioning the eternal questions of life and death!**'

"**Fantastic, entertaining read.**"
"**Absolutely loved this book.** It hooks you in **from the start, triggers your imagination and keeps you entertained** with great references to north east locations throughout. **Definitely recommend this book to anyone who enjoys science fiction, horror or just an entertaining read.**"

RICHARDVALANGA
BLIND VISION

To see the evil dead is a curse...

It begins with the Roman exploratore Stasius Tenebris and the Calicem Tenebris (the Dark Chalice) - a vessel of evil that is brought back to life years later by Ethan Chance, a young man who was cruelly blinded by falling into an ancient Roman well when he was nine.

Was it an accident or did the spirits in the well choose Ethan for a reason? ...the Calicem Tenebris restores his sight but at a price.

This is the story of the chalice and the village called Darwell and the dark fate awaiting its inhabitants at the Festival of Healing.

Can Ethan, his friends and a knight from the Crusades save the day or is Darwell doomed to forever serve those who worship Mars, the Roman God of War.

'**Blindingly good book**'
This is the second book by Richard Valanga I have read and it's even better than his first, Complex Heaven. **If, like me, you enjoy fantasy novels that you can't put down then this author is for you.**
- Mick Averre.

'**Brilliant!**'
'Although "Blind Vision" is primarily aimed at young adult readers I still thoroughly enjoyed this book, I was drawn into it from the very first

page with **great characters and a truly intriguing dark supernatural story line**. Set in 2 time frames- present day and fantasy Roman/Crusaders the story comes together brilliantly in a very detailed and fascinating way.'

'**Richard Valanga is a great writer who has a fantastic imagination and I would happily recommend "Blind Vision" to readers of any age - you won't be disappointed!**'

'**The end is very exciting.** You can feel the tension in the air. You can't put the book down. You just want to read faster and faster to find out what's going to happen. It is absolutely amazing. **One of the best books I have ever read**.' – A Young Adult reader.

RICHARDVALANGA
THE LAST ANGEL

When the unbelievable finally happens, who will be the one who will save us all?

Heaven is no more. All the Angelic have gone and the world is about to be consumed by a Dark Conscious, pure evil as old as time itself.

After thousands of years of exile, one of the banished Angelic finally returns to Earth.

Is he the last angel? Or are their others like him who will join him in the fight against the inevitable darkness that threatens the world of the living.

First reactions...

"I have just started reading The Last Angel **and I am totally gripped!**"

"Cracking!"

THE MUSIC OF FAMILY
AND ME
a memoir
RICHARDVALANGA

Family were an English underground progressive rock band of the late sixties and early seventies. Brilliant, eclectic, original and unique are just some of the words that describe Family, a band fronted by the amazing singer songwriter called Roger Chapman who still continues to excite people today with his excellent solo career, check out his latest brilliant album called Life In The Pond.

In this memoir, I use the music of Family as a vehicle to journey back in time as I review each album and each song to see what memories they open up for me. I really hope that you enjoy this personal trip which I primarily wrote for my son James. For me, Family were the best, they produced music like no other, it is as simple as that.

revisit, review, recall

"I have to say **I feel humbled** in a big headed sort of way. Anyway, tell Richard it's great to read 50/100 pages of great reviews & **I appreciate it very much.** If he could send me some copies when published, I'll circulate to the people who I think & hopefully himself count. Again thanx very much, **a real honour.** Cheers, **Roger Chapman.**"

"Cheers & must say **love the idea** as it also brings me back long forgotten memories good & bad. - **Roger Chapman.**"

Wow!!! I am now starting the chapter about Family's 2nd LP, "Entertainment." What is so nice to read is the author's memories juxtapositioned next to his discussion of the music and the times in his life and world make this **such a warm, inviting reading experience.** This combination engages me on diferent levels. Even better, Richard Valanga's book causes me to reach for the CD'S that he is focussing on. Music is a universal language. So is the lexiconic message in words. **This gentleman does this exquisitely!!**
I would most highly recommend this book. Especially, if you loved the band Family and the music of Roger Chapman. (By the way, Roger's new CD, at 79 years young, **"Life in the Pond"** is also an incredible slick of **fabulous Music of the highest order**.)
David Freshman.

What a great book to read about the songs of **Family**, the British band. This band operated on so many different musical levels and styles! **Richard Valanga's work is so unique in that it juxtapositions his life and how the songs and music of Family made him feel.** This book is a fast read with **great insights** and defining understandings of the inner workings of the band and their music.

With **great details** explained by Mr. **Roger Chapman**, the lead singer/lyricist in the iconic band, the veracity and meanings become all the more **focussed and clear.**

A great book to have! Great work Mr. Valanga!
David Freshman.

I've had the privilege to read this before it went to print, and I have to say that **I am mightily impressed by this tome, to the extent that I couldn't put it down!**

This book is different from so many other Rock biographies in so much that it connects Valanga the writer to whatever he was doing at the time, and it does this in a song by song album way. So not only do you get a history of the writer as he came of age he carefully juxtaposes his life with the music of Family as it came out of the gramophone round a friend's house, or the radio at work, or in concert in Sunderland - **quite clever really...**
Simon Boxall.

Great Book
It was about time someone wrote a book about Family! Along with the Beatles and Led Zeppelin they were one of the most influential in my career as a musician. It gives **a great insight into the band and it's music. Fantastic writing** from someone who undoubtably loved Family as much (if not more) as I do.
It's a must have for me!
Paul Thompson - Roxy Music.

A mixture of 'High Fidelity' and '31 Songs' THE MUSIC OF FAMILY AND ME is **a very readable tale of fandom, obsession and heartache.** It is a great example of what music means, not only for teenagers but to people of any age!
Marc Andelane.

A great read

Love this book. As a lifetime fan of Family it's great to relate back to the memories of the group and the legacy of the music. Richard used his memories of the group to paint a .picture of the albums and the live gigs I could easily relate to. **A lovely nostalgic trip back.**
Tony Upton.

Entertainment
Excellent read chronological review of the great band FAMILY. **Well done Richard** got me to play all the albums again. **Thank you.**
Eddy.

Excellent!
I **really enjoyed reading this book** and reminiscing about my favourite band and their songs.
Mr Paul D Barnett.

Great Family read
Richard **takes us through every album** release and I'm right there with him.
David Jeanes.

A **fantastic** read from one of the finest rock bands Britain produced.
John Atkinson.

Evocative Memoir of a Great Band
Never saw Family perform live since I was a USA midwestern boy/man. But **this personal memoir helps evoke what being there in the UK in those heady days would have felt like.**
Richard L Giovanoni.

A criminally neglected band from the 70s gets it due - 5 STARS
In the early 70s a friend from my high school years Mike Green came back from a hitch-hiking trip he made through England. As was common back in the day Mike and I talked music when we got together, specifically we talked about the music scene in England this time. Mike knew I loved the bands Yes and Jethro Tull, " Yeah, Yes and Tull are big in England like here in the States", he mentioned. He went on, "But you know what? There is a different scene going on in England than here." A band called the Move is big "over there" he told me and there is this other group that is bigger than all of these... Mike loans me a record by

this band that goes by the name Family, the record is FEARLESS. I notice the album has this multi-leaf cover, that is pretty novel, and I take it home and put it on with no expectations (the best way there is to listen to a new record if you ask me) and no previous knowledge of the band. Putting side 2 on first (a habit of mine) Take Your Partners spills into my room from my console tv/ record player combo I had at the time. There is this squiggly, funky electronic intro first, then the percussion starts slowly kicking in and with the first minute of Take Your Partners my consciousness takes immediately to "something" in this music, others have called the experience the sound of surprise (always a good thing to adventurous listeners). It was playful, syncopated and very English in a way I had yet experienced at the time.

So it went over the years with each of their albums. Each one with a different vibe that drew me in in some way as Take Your Partners and the rest of FEARLESS had. I played Family to friends who came by my place, but I can't recall anyone being all that impressed with them back in the day. Undaunted and in some way emboldened it made their music more endearing to me, they became one of "my" bands. ♥

Fast forward to almost 50 years later I come across the Facebook group Richard Valanga leads - **Family With Roger Chapman Appreciation Society. There I found the music I love by Family**, the solo music of Roger Chapman and other members of the band cast in a new light. **Here were droves of mostly folks from the British Isles who took for granted all along that Family was the greatest band ever.** I was like Dorothy landing in Oz.😊 I love the insights into a favorite band of mine from fans who were boots on the ground back in the day. So many stories from the past as well as current heads ups to recent developments with the band and members. Not the least of which came from the current book's author Richard Valanga.

With this as a lead in I was all set for Richard's book THE MUSIC OF FAMILY AND ME. ♥ **This is not Richard's first book and clearly is a labour of love.** The hours I shared with friends like Mike Green at the beginning of this review, hours talking about music come back in rich ways as **Richard shares his love for the music of Family. This was unexpectedly and especially endearing about this memoir.** Check it out. Doesn't matter if you are a die-hard fan or a complete and total novice like I was in 1972. Read the book and re-hear the music in tandem; or hear the music fresh to your ears and go the book for a clear perspective that Richard lends. **Either way this book is a winner.**
Jeff Gifford.

Like being in the pub with a friend...
Like the author I first saw Family back in 1971 and like the author my father fought at Kohima (one of the bloodiest battles of WW2). Back then, when your mate got a new album and before you got chance to get together to listen to it, erstwhile chum would describe the songs to you :) This review and recollections of Family's canon of music is like being down the pub with your friend talking about the latest music that you have heard. To be picky, the downside is that the book is self-published and suffers the vagaries of sending a file off for printing - no matter how hard you try the pagination etc is going to get a bit weird. But that is being picky. A great read...and if you are not familiar with Family then you should be...jazzy, rhythmically interesting, wonderful melodies and musicianship. In addition Roger Chapman wrote thoughtful well constructed lyrics. Live, they were on another planet...Chapman terrifying!
Kim38

RICHARDVALANGA
THE NEXT REALITY

To get to Heaven
You have to go through Hell

The Blue Ripple is an anomaly of nature that will transfer your mind to another reality.

A young man risks the Ripple to see the woman he had loved and had died in his reality.

The man is accidentally joined by investigator Nick Thorn in a strange twist of fate that makes them battle the dangers of a different world together.

Murder, abduction and dark eroticism await the two men in the deadly and vicious next reality.

Will love prevail?

Or was the journey a leap of faith too far?

RICHARDVALANGA

BLOOD MIRACLE

A theological mystery thriller.

A young man with amnesia finds himself in an isolated farmhouse during an unnatural heavy snowstorm. Where is he, who is he? Mysterious dreams, sudden hallucinations, enigmatic artworks, contemporary music, strange marble statues, compelling intriguing books, famous artists and an obsessive author become part of the metaphysical puzzle that builds in intensity day by day, threatening the young man's sanity as the answer to the mystery of who he is becomes increasingly crucial. Will Churchyard Farm experience a miracle; can the stranded, lost young man's sanity and his fragile soul be saved?

RICHARDVALANGA
DAY OF THE ROMAN

They all thought that the story of the Festival of Healing had been concluded.

But the shadow of evil is back in the northern town of Darwell, determined to find the Sword of Pluto, a sword that could determine the future of the world.

Ethan Chance is blind and has gone missing and his family and friends are worried. Ethan has a 'Blind Vision' that is capable of seeing pure evil and the living dead but now this power has mutated.

Where is Ethan and what is is his connection to the Sword of Pluto and the Shield of Saturn?

Can Ethan's friend, Adam Sunderland and an old Viking spirit called Ragnar save Darwell once again from the threatening forces of the ancient Roman AGOTE, who want to send the world back in time?

RICHARD VALANGA
THE MUSIC OF ROXY MUSIC
ENO AND ME
a memoir

Inspired by the critical success of my Music of Family memoir, I decided to continue with a Roxy Music Eno memoir which sort of made sense to my personal time-line, the inclusion of my formative art college years.

So I drifted back to those golden years aided by the incredible music of Roxy Music and Brian Eno which was a vehicle to re-ignite my memories, a key to unlock those dormant thoughts...

We cannot go back but we can remember, the what ifs, the if only's, the heartache and joys of a young life and I always needed something to get me through the dark times and music was that something, a shining light of hope that has never faded.

Once again, this memoir is for my son James, a little insight into the life of his father when he was a young man so any unfavourable critical response to this book will mean absolutely nothing to me, all I can hope is that you do enjoy this memoir and I am sure that the music of Roxy Music and Eno will bring back memorable moments for you too.

Viva Roxy, viva Eno!

"Thanks for the memories!"
"I picked up the Sunderland vampire's latest edition of him. Devoured it in two sittings and thoroughly enjoyed it. I was more interested in Richard's life than the Roxy/Eno bits, although I was obviously into those too. I figure there's a couple of years between us and NE common ground, so a lot of it felt really familiar - from the plastic Beatles wig to the strangeness of leaving hyem for college. Thank you for sharing your memories and helping me relive mine. X"

"If you were present at the time, a great read, and even if you weren't!"
"Brought back so many memories of an amazing time in the music world. If you're a Roxy Music fan this is a must have. I lived in London at the time but can relate to so much of what Richard writes about.
Great stuff and also fascinating insight to the authors life."

"Another rapid page turner from the 21st century master of thrillers/nostalgia."
"I loved the reviews of songs, and memories of the writers younger days, it made me think I'd been there although I'm a bit younger and located miles away."

Printed in Poland
by Amazon Fulfillment
Poland Sp. z o.o., Wrocław
02 March 2023

5c48bb3c-1f60-4203-9c4d-1b0d7eef920eR02